How To Do Magic:

Professional effects
for beginners

Matt Walker

First published in Great Britain in 2020 by Matt Walker

Photos by Annabel Walker

www.walkerproductions.co.uk

Twitter: @_mattwalker
Facebook Page: @mattwalkerproductions
Instagram: walkerproductions.co.uk

Also by Matt Walker:

<u>OTHER MAGIC TITLES</u>

Mercury: A Book Test (under pseudonym LM Wood)

<u>NOVELS</u>

The Beyond
There is a world beyond this one, a land of ghosts.
And somehow I'm stuck there.

Shark Bait
A government hitman. A family of drug pushers.
And a loan shark picks on the wrong guy.

Memories Unspeakable
A secret. A memory that needs to be shared.
And those who will kill to keep it hidden.

<u>SHEET MUSIC TITLES</u>

Favourite Children's Songs For Piano
More Favourite Children's Songs For Piano
Favourite Children's Songs For Piano… & More!
Favourite Children's Classics For Piano
Favourite Children's Christmas For Piano
Light & Shade (assorted compositions)
American Folk Songs: Favorite Melodies For Really Easy Piano
Nursery Rhymes: Favourite Melodies For Really Easy Piano
Christmas Favourites: Favourite Melodies For Really Easy Piano

CONTENTS

Sleights are in *italics*. Effects are in **bold**.

INTRODUCTION

I have been performing and creating magic for nearly twenty years. Over that time I have learnt a very important point: the strongest effects are not necessarily the most complicated or difficult to perform.

Simple tricks can be just as effective, just as miraculous, just as strong.

The first few tricks are very basic, in order to ease you into performing. The rest are straight out of my professional repertoire. When performed with fluency and flair, they are guaranteed to mystify and amaze.

We will start with the most basic tricks, requiring the least amount of work, and as we progress through the book the tricks will get more challenging (and rewarding) to perform.

Even though these first few effects can be learnt with relative ease, it is vital to practise them thoroughly before performing them for anyone. Make sure you are completely confident before you perform and you are sure of success.

Magic goes back hundreds of years. We don't know who invented many of the card and coin sleights used by magicians today, but I have tried to credit where possible. The vast majority of the effects in this book are of my own creation, built on the foundations laid by countless magicians throughout the centuries.

I hope you enjoy the start of your magical journey.

Matt Walker

<u>SECTION ONE</u>

BASIC CARD HANDLING

THE DECK OF CARDS

Card magic is very popular – probably the most popular genre of magic. Many people still play card games, and most people have a pack of cards lying about their house. Let us quickly discuss the deck of cards.

There are 52 cards, divided into 4 suits. The 4 suits are *spades, clubs, hearts* and *diamonds*. The hearts and diamonds are red cards, the spades and clubs are black cards. It is pretty self explanatory as to which suit is which, although some people (children especially) might not remember 'clubs' and call them 'trees' or 'cauliflowers' instead. Please call them *clubs*. Thank you.

There are number cards and picture cards. The number cards are self explanatory, and run from 2 through 10. The picture cards are the following: Ace (which usually stands for the number 1), Jack (number 11), Queen (12) and King (13). The picture cards have *A, J, Q* or *K* in their corners instead of numbers.

When we say *face-up*, we mean that the card's number or picture is displayed. When we say *face-down*, the back of the card is displayed. The backs of the playing cards can be many colours, but the most common are red and blue.

There are often two jokers in the pack, also, which are not used in card games but can be included in effects.

HANDLING THE PACK

The deck of cards is usually held in the left hand, with the thumb along one side, three fingers along the other, and the index finger at the front.

Look at the picture opposite. This is known as the *Mechanic's Grip*, and is the default position for handling the pack.

Practise holding the pack in this way until it feels completely natural.

<u>Dealing the cards</u> is another very basic skill, and you need to be comfortable doing so before we can begin learning effects.

Hold the pack in your left hand in mechanic's grip, as the previous page. Your left thumb pushes the top card over to the right, and your right hand takes it and places it on the table, face-down. Repeat the motion, dealing the cards one on top of the other into a pile on the table. Okay? Good.

<u>Cutting the deck:</u> When we say *cut the cards*, we don't mean attack the deck with a pair of scissors. Cutting simply involves picking up a block of cards from the top of the deck (usually about half the pack) and putting it down next to the remaining cards. So you end up with two piles on the table, next to each other.

Completing the cut involves picking up the bottom half and putting it on top of the other pile (the former top half). This ensures that whatever cards were at the top of the deck are now buried in the middle.

<u>Shuffling:</u> There are different types of card shuffle, and all involve mixing up the cards. Firstly we will learn the basic *overhand* shuffle, but later on we will also look at the riffle shuffle and various false shuffles too.

Pic 1

For the overhand shuffle, begin with the pack held at 90 degrees in your right hand, by the short edges, as in the opposite **pic 1**. This is called the *Biddle grip*. Your left hand is held palm up, to catch the cards.

Lower the deck to your left hand and let a small packet drop from the top of it, onto your left fingers. Now raise your right hand, leaving the small packet behind, held upright by your left fingers (**pic 2**). The right hand retains the rest of the deck.

Pic 2

The cards now on top of the packet in your right hand (marked with an **X** in pic 2) are now going to be deposited on top of (to the left of) the small packet in your left hand.

Repeat the previous chopping motion, bringing your right hand down to your left palm, this time in front of (to the left of) the small packet already held against your left fingers. Drop off another small packet (from those cards marked with an **X**) and raise the remaining cards again.

Repeat the chopping motion, depositing another small packet on top of the previous one, and so on, until all the cards have been transferred from your right hand to your left, and are jumbled up.

Practise this overhand shuffle until you are familiar with it. You can do the first few tricks in this book without, put start practising now so you are completely comfortable with it when required.

Effect 1:

<u>TWINS</u>

Non-identical twins would be a more accurate name. The workings of this effect date from the early 1800s at least. It is simple but effective.

Effect: The spectator deals a random number of cards, as many as they like, and a red queen is inserted into the deck at that chosen place. The process is repeated, and magically those red queens find their sisters, the two black queens.

Method: Simple, but effective. You can deal the cards yourself, asking the spectator to say "stop" whenever they wish, or you can let the spectator deal the cards, stopping whenever they wish.

There is a setup. Before you begin, take out all the queens. Put one black queen on the bottom of the pack and the other black queen on top. Leave the two red queens face-up on the table. You are ready to begin.

Draw the spectator's attention to the two red queens lying face-up on the table. "Hey, look at these red queens just lying here face-up on the table." The spectator sees them. "Which queen is the more attractive, do you think?"

The spectator doesn't know what to say to that.

"Here, take the deck of cards." You hand the deck to the spectator. "Deal some cards from the top of the deck into a pile. Stop whenever you feel like it."

If the spectator starts dealing from the bottom of the pack (which has happened to me before), ask them where they went to school, take the pack off them and deal the cards yourself, asking them to say "stop".

You will notice that the first card dealt is the top card of the deck, which is one of the black queens. This card gets put down first, with the other cards dealt on top of it. It doesn't matter how many cards are dealt - the spectator can deal 5 or 25 – the *bottom* card of the packet just dealt will always be the black queen.

After the spectator has stopped dealing (or stopped you), take one of the red queens lying face-up on the table. Place it **face-up** on the little packet of cards the spectator has just dealt.

Now pick up the rest of the deck. Remember, the bottom card is the *other* black queen. Put this block of cards, as one, face-down on top of the face-up red queen (which is on top of the pile of cards dealt by the spectator). This puts the red queen and the black queen face-to-face in the middle of the deck.

Now pick up the **entire** pack. You are going to repeat the previous steps. Have the spectator deal some cards from the top of the deck and stop whenever they wish. Place the other red queen face-up on the little tabled packet. Then put the rest of the deck (which has the other black queen on the bottom, remember) on top of that face-up red queen.

Once again, the red queen and black queen are squashed together face-to-face.

"Remember," you say, "you dealt as many cards as you wanted. You could have stopped at any time. And we put the red queens into the deck at the places you chose. Now look…"

With your right hand, spread the pack across the table like the pictures below. You push with your right index and middle fingers, keeping the deck square with the others. This will take some practise to achieve an even spread.

 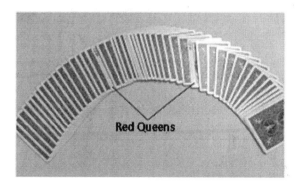

Notice the two face-up red queens in the spread. The cards directly to the right of them (on top of them, face-to-face with them) are the black queens. With two fingers, pull out the first pair of queens, one finger on the face-up red queen and the other on the face-down black queen. Then repeat with the other pair.

"You put the red queens into the deck at places you chose, and you have found the two black queens, their sisters."

Effect 2:

BUM DEAL ACE ASSEMBLY

There are lots of different ace assembly effects. This is my version. It's simple but very effective. It uses the same dealing principle as the previous trick. I originally named this 'Bottom Deal Ace Assembly', because the story hinges on the *bottom deal*, but Bum Deal is funnier, doncha think?

Method: Have the four aces on top and the four kings on the bottom of the deck. At the start of the performance, turn the pack face-up and spread the lower half (the half on the right) to show the four kings on the bottom to the spectators. "Gamblers and card sharks will often *bottom deal* cards, which is when you apparently deal a card from the top of the deck, as normal, but you actually deal the *bottom* card. As you can see, I have the four kings on the bottom of the deck." Make sure you don't flash the four aces on the top!

Turn the deck over, face-down. "I'm going to deal four piles into the middle of the table…" Deal the top four cards (the aces) face-down across the table. They do NOT go on top of each other; you deal them next to each other, as if dealing a hand to four players. "And the fifth card I will bottom deal to myself."

You are now going to bottom deal the bottom card and put it in front of you. "I'll do it in slow motion." Keep your thumb on top of the deck, and very slowly peel off the bottom (king) with your right fingers and put it in front of you. Notice that you don't need to be able to perform the *actual* bottom deal. You don't need to fool anyone. Just pretend that you can, okay? The table will look like the picture below, from your point of view.

Now repeat the previous steps: deal cards from the top onto the four cards (aces) in the middle, and then bottom deal in slow motion the second king in front of yourself. Repeat two more times. You'll end up with the four kings in front of you, and four packets in the middle with an ace on the bottom of each.

Turn your four kings over. "As you can see, I've dealt myself four kings – a very strong hand!" Push the kings away to one side. Now pick up each pile from the centre and replace them onto the deck, one at a time, one on top of the other. This leaves the top of the deck in this position: 3 cards, ACE, 3 cards, ACE, 3 cards, ACE, 3 cards, ACE. You say, "Now, I had to cheat to deal myself four kings. Some people don't need to cheat. They have luck on their side." Hand the deck to the spectator. "Deal <u>three</u> piles into the middle and the <u>fourth</u> pile to yourself." Mime the deal if needs be. You'll notice every fourth card, which they deal to themselves, is an ace. After they've dealt all four cards out tell them to stop and check their hand. They'll be astonished to see the four aces.

Effect 3:

CARD PREDICTION

This is a simple feat of mentalism I came up with. It uses the same deal control as *TWINS*, and also something called the *Magician's Force*. There are a number of different presentations.

Effect: The magician writes a prediction on a piece of paper, screws it up into a ball and leaves it in plain sight. The spectator chooses a card after a free dealing process. The magician reveals the prediction. The cards match.

Method: This trick is an introduction to the world of *forces*. The card that the spectator ends up choosing has been forced upon them by the magician. They couldn't have picked any other. You will find other card forces later on in the book, but this is an easy one to begin with.

First, have the card you wish to force (the force card) on top of the deck. Let's say it's the 6 of hearts. This is the card the spectator will end up with, but of course they believe they have a free choice.

Announce that you are writing a prediction on a piece of paper. Write '6 of hearts' down, secretly, screw the paper up into a ball and leave it on the table in full view.

Now give the deck to the spectator. Ask them to deal any number of cards face-down into a pile. You will notice that the force card, the 6 of hearts, gets put down first and becomes the bottom card of the packet. If you're worried about them messing up the deal, deal the cards yourself, getting the spectator to say "stop."

When you have a little packet of cards, discard the rest of the deck as you don't need it any longer. Get the spectator to pick up the packet from the table and to deal it into two piles. Remember that the bottom card of the packet in their hand is the 6 of hearts. This means that the *last card* the spectator puts down will be the 6 of hearts. Make sure you notice which pile it ends up on.

Now pick up the top cards of the two piles, one in each hand, keeping them face-down. Let's say that you know the 6 of hearts is in your left hand. You are now going to use the magician's force, ensuring the spectator ends up picking the 6 of hearts.

You do NOT say, "Choose one of the cards." You say, "*Take* one of the cards in my hand," holding them out. What you do next depends on which card they take.

If they take the card in your left hand, the 6 of hearts, all well and good. Discard the other card and say, "Great. Have a look and tell everyone what you picked."

If they take the card in your right hand (the 'wrong' card) that's fine too. All you say is, "Okay, great. That leaves us with *this* card." The card in your left hand, which of course is the 6 of hearts.

So it doesn't matter which card they take; you bend it in your favour. They either take the 6 of hearts, or they take the other card, which *leaves* the 6 of hearts, as if that were the point all along.

That is why you say "take a card" and not "choose a card." Instruct them to reveal what is written on the screwed up bit of paper.

Other presentations:

1) Instead of having the force card on top at the very start, you could do it this way. Give them the pack to shuffle. After they've shuffled, take the pack back and look through it, shifting the cards between your hands. You can do this under the guise of: "Oh no... did I leave the jokers in there? No we're okay." Or simply, "I'm just going to look through the pack for a card that jumps out at me. Mmmm, yes. *This* one."

Of course, what you're really doing is having a look at what the top card is, which will be the one furthest on your left. That is the card that ends up forced on the spectator. After looking through the shuffled pack and noting the top card, return the deck to the table and write it down on the paper. Then proceed with the effect.

2) For this presentation you'll need to have the top card already known, so the spectator won't be able to shuffle the deck. Let's imagine it's the 6 of hearts. Instead of writing your prediction on a piece of paper, use a pad of post-its.

Pic 1

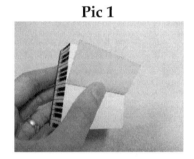

Beforehand, secretly, write 6 of hearts on a post-it. Now whilst it's still attached, fold the paper in half, bottom edge *up* (**pic 1**). Now detach it and stick it *under* the new top post-it, so it's hidden (**pic 2**).

Pic 2

At the start of the trick, ask the spectator for a prediction. Imagine they say king of clubs. Openly write *king of clubs* on the top post-it so they can see. Have the block of post-its on the table whilst you do this. The folded post-it is completely hidden.

After you've written it, pick up the post-it block. Fold up the top sheet, bottom to top, exposing the pre-folded sheet below – make sure the spectators can't see! Now pull off this pre-folded post-it with 6 of hearts written on it – the one you prepared earlier.

The spectators think you hold a folded post-it with king of clubs written on it, when really you hold one with the 6 of hearts.

Discard the post-it block, preferably in a pocket. Make sure no one can see the folded up king of clubs sheet still attached.

Fold the 6 of hearts post-it one last time and leave it on the table, or give it to the spectator that chose the king of clubs.

Proceed with the effect.

When the 6 of hearts has been chosen (forced) at the end, look a bit stumped. "Hmm," you say. "Didn't you say the king of clubs?"

The spectator thinks you're blaming him for the failure of the trick and probably thinks you're being a bit unfair.

"No problem!" you continue. "Look at the post-it. What does it say?"

"Well golly-gosh," everyone answers in perfect unison.

Effect 4:

<u>ANOTHER ACE ASSEMBLY</u>

The effect is much the same as the previous assembly, but with a different presentation. It uses a four-choice magician's force.

Effect: The spectator cuts and deals the pack into four separate piles, and an ace magically appears at the top of each one.

Method: Start with the four aces on the bottom of the deck. Obviously do not point out this setup to the spectator. If you can riffle shuffle the cards, maintaining the bottom four aces in position by letting them fall first, do that. If not, don't worry. (You can learn the riffle shuffle on page 30).

So, the deck is in front of the spectator. Ask them to cut the pack in half. If they pick it up and try to rip it in two like a strongman tearing apart a phonebook (no joke, this has happened to me before), demonstrate what cutting the pack involves.

So they cut the pack in half, and you have two piles sitting in the middle of the table. You MUST remember where the aces are and keep track of them at all times. It isn't too tricky. Just keep track of the very bottom of the deck.

Now get them to cut these two piles in half again, so you end up with a row of four piles on the table. Again, don't lose the aces! They will almost always be at the bottom of one of the two inner piles, not the outer ones.

Now ask the spectator to deal some cards from the piles into the middle, making a fifth pile in front of you. They can take cards from any of the piles just as long as they deal one at a time. Stop them when they've dealt maybe ten or twelve cards. If you fear the aces' pile is getting low and they may start dealing aces, stop them immediately.

The table in front of you will look something like this: four piles in a row in front of the spectator, and a smaller packet in the middle, which has been dealt by the spectator from any of the four piles.

Let's imagine the aces are at the bottom of the pile marked with the letter **C**.

You are now going to perform a four-choice magician's force. The spectator will end up 'choosing' the pile with the four aces at the bottom (the pile marked **C** in this example), but in reality they have no choice at all. You force it upon them.

You say, "Touch two of the piles in front of you." You do NOT say "choose two of the piles."

If one of the piles they touch is the aces' pile (**C**) then you say, "Okay, you keep those two," and move the *other* two piles into the middle, next to the smaller packet. For example, if they touch piles **A** and **C**, then you move piles **B** and **D**. If they touch piles **B** and **C**, then you move piles **A** and **D**. If they touch piles **D** and **C**, then you move piles **A** and **B**.

If they do not touch the aces' pile (i.e. they touch piles **A** and **B**, or **A** and **D**, or **B** and **D**) then you say, "Okay, we'll bring them into the middle." And you move the piles they touched into the middle next to the smaller packet.

It doesn't matter which piles they touch, they are always left with the aces' pile still in front of them. Your response is either, "Okay, we keep the ones you touched in front of you," (if they touch the aces) **OR** "Okay, we'll move the ones you touched into the middle" (if they don't touch the aces).

It is complicated to explain but quite simple in practise.

So, you will be in this position: three piles in the middle of the table, and two still in front of the spectator, one of which has the aces at the bottom. Now say to the spectator, "Pick up one of the piles still in front of you."

If they pick up the aces' pile, fine. Leave them holding it and slide the remaining pile towards you into the middle, making a row of four packets.

If they pick up the other pile and leave the one with the aces on the table, that's fine too. Simply reach out and take the pile they're holding out of their hand. Put it in the middle next to the other three, making a row of four, leaving the aces' pile still in front of them on the table. It doesn't matter what they do, they are always left with the aces' pile.

So you are now in this position: a row of four piles in the middle of the table. And the pile with the aces at the bottom is either still in front of the spectator or in their hand.

Now simply ask them to take the pile they're left with and to deal the cards one at a time across the four piles in the middle. Demonstrate with invisible cards. They must NOT deal randomly. They must deal in order, like this: A, B, C, D - A, B, C, D – A, B, C, D etc.

This ensures the four bottom cards (the four aces) end up on the top of each pile. Remind them what happened. They cut the deck, into four. They dealt cards into the middle. They chose which piles to move, and which to deal with. It really is an astonishing effect.

THE KEY CARD PRINCIPLE

The key card principle can be used whenever the deck is cut. Look at the bottom card of the deck and remember it. Let's say it is the 4 of clubs. Now, still holding the pack in your left hand, cut the top half to the table.

Look at the top card of the pile in your hand. This is the card you cut to. Let's say it's the ace of spades. Instead of putting it back on the pile in your hand, put it on top of the packet on the table. Then put the cards in your hand on top of that.

Notice what happened? The 4 of clubs (the bottom card of the deck) has been placed on top of the card you cut to (the ace of spades).

Now if you pick up the deck and look through it, you will find that the 4 of clubs is just behind (to the left of) the ace of spades. And thus, if you hadn't known the identity of the ace of spades you would have been able to work it out, because it is the card next to (to the right of) the key card, the 4 of clubs.

Key Card

Of course, you can do a simple card location using the above method. Have the spectator shuffle the pack, and when you take it back glimpse the bottom card. Ask a spectator to lift off and table the top half. Then they look at the card they cut to, then put it on the tabled packet. Place your half on top of that tabled pile and then you can find out what the spectator's card was as before. It will be to the right of the key card you glimpsed at the start.

Just searching through the pack and picking out the spectator's card isn't the best of effects, however. So here are a couple of better ones.

Effect 5:

<u>DO AS I DO</u>

This is a very popular effect dating back over a hundred years, with credit due to Jean Hugard, Frederick Braue and others. It was also my nan's favourite trick. Once I tried to teach it her as a Christmas present, but she couldn't understand it. Hopefully you'll have more success, because you're probably not as old as she was.

Effect: Two decks are used, one for the magician and one for the spectator. The cards are shuffled. You both cut to a card and remember it. It turns out that the cards match.

Method: Have two packs of cards, preferably with different coloured backs (although this is not essential). The most common coloured backs are red and blue, so this is what we will assume.

The spectator should be sitting opposite you at a table. Let them choose which pack they want to use. Let's say they choose the red pack. Hand it to them and keep the blue pack for yourself.

"We will be using two decks," you say, which should be apparent. "And I want you to do as I do (which also happens to be the name of the trick). I want you to shuffle the cards when I shuffle, and cut when I cut. Can you do that? Good. Now, if we both do exactly the same thing, we should get the same result, should we not?"

The spectator isn't overly convinced by this logic, but never mind.

"Shuffle your pack of cards," you say, whilst shuffling your own blue pack. Use the overhand shuffle.

The spectator shuffles their cards.

"Okay, now let's swap packs. You shuffle my deck and I'll shuffle yours."

You swap decks, and you shuffle the red pack whilst the spectator shuffles the blue pack. After completing the shuffle, you need to glimpse the bottom card of the spectator's red deck. It shouldn't be too difficult; you have it in your hands. If you wish you can shuffle the pack with the faces showing. Let's say the bottom card is the 3 of spades.

"Okay, the decks are thoroughly shuffled. Let's swap back."

You give the spectator back their red pack, and you take back your blue pack. Put it on the table in front of you and instruct the spectator to do the same with their own deck. "Now we cut the cards."

Take off about half the cards from the top of your blue deck and put them a little off to the right.

Make sure the spectator does the same. The bottom half (3 of spades on the very bottom) is in front of them, and they'll put the top half to one side.

"Now look at the card you cut to."

This is the card on the pile directly in front of you. The spectator needs to look at the card on top of the pile directly in front of them (the one with the 3 of spades on the bottom).

You look at your card and instantly forget it. As you look at it, say *3 of spades* to yourself over and over, because that's the only card you need to remember.

Instruct the spectator to remember their card, however. It is not good when a spectator forgets what their card is.

"Remembered it?" you say. "Now put it on *this* pile…" and you put the card in your hand on the pile to your right. You do NOT put it back on the pile in front of you, which is where you picked it up from.

Make sure the spectator puts their card on the other pile too.

"Now we bury it in the middle of the deck."

Pick up the pile in front of you and put it on top of the other pile, which has your 'chosen card' on top (even though you can't remember what it is).

The spectator needs to pick up the pile in front of them, which has the 3 of spades on the bottom, remember. When they put this pile on top of the other one, the 3 of spades goes directly on top of their chosen card.

"Now I am going to find my card in your deck and you are going to find your card in my deck. Let's swap again."

You swap decks again. Now all you need to do it find the 3 of spades in the spectator's red deck, and their chosen card will be the one just to the right of it. Let's say their chosen card was the 7 of hearts. You pick it out and put it face down on the table, pretending this is the card you cut to in your own deck.

The spectator, of course, will find the 7 of hearts in the blue deck and pick it out. Reveal that both cards match.

Effect 6:

<u>CARD SENSE</u>

You can turn the *back* of a card into a key card also. Take out any card and turn it face down. Notice the white border. Put a pencil dot in the top left and bottom right corners. You have turned this card into a blind key card.

Effect: A card is selected and replaced. You use your mentalist powers to select three cards from the deck and place them face down on the table. The spectator picks one. It is their chosen card.

Method: Have the blind key card on the bottom of the deck. Now you're going to give the deck an overhand shuffle whilst retaining the bottom key card in position. Do so thus: as you peel off each packet from the top of the deck, your left fingers press against the bottom card (the blind key card). When you lift the deck with your right hand, your left fingers slide the bottom card off to the back of the small packet in your left hand. And this is repeated every time you lift your right hand – your left fingers keep the bottom card in place. Try it now and see how easy it is.

Spread the pack out and let the spectator pick any card. Instruct them to remember it. Now cut off half the cards and offer the top half out to the spectator with your right hand. "Put it back," you say, and they put their chosen card on top of that packet.

Now put the bottom half (the cards remaining in your left hand) on top of the pile in your right. The blind key card goes directly on top of the spectator's chosen card.

Put the deck on the table and leave it for a few moments as you discuss how your psychic abilities work. The spectators will notice that the card is really lost in the middle of the deck, and you're not holding its position or any of the other dodgy sleight of hand stuff we will learn later on.

Pick the deck back up and say you are going to try and sense which card the spectator chose. Run through the deck, holding it face-down. Take out a random card and put it on the table, face-down. "Mmm, I think that one called out to me," you say, which is a big fat lie.

Watch out for the blind key card. It will have the pencil dot in the top left corner. And remember it went on *top* of the spectator's chosen card, so when you find the key card the spectator's card will be underneath it, to the left.

When you locate the spectator's chosen card remove it and put it on the table face-down. Then take out another random card and put it with the others. Put the deck aside.

So you have three face-down cards on the table, and one of them is the spectator's card. Do remember which one it is, won't you.

Now you are going to execute a three card magician's force.

Ask the spectator to touch one of the cards. If they touch the chosen card, great. Ask them to name their chosen card and then turn over the card on the table.

If they touch one of the other two, that's fine as well. Scoot it aside and then pick up the remaining two cards (the ones the spectator did NOT touch, one of which, of course, is their chosen card). Ask them to take a card. If they take the chosen card, great. If they take the other, you say, "Okay, that leaves us with *this* card," which is the chosen card.

The technique is exactly the same as at the end of **CARD PREDICTION** on page 11.

This effect is made even stronger by the fact that the magician never sees any of the faces until the very last moment, when the chosen card is turned over.

SECTION TWO

THE GLIDE

THE GLIDE

In the last section, the effects only needed an understanding of dealing, cutting, shuffling, and an important concept known as the *magician's force*. We are now going to learn our first proper card sleight.

The glide is a simple yet powerful tool. The spectator thinks you take one card when you really take another.

Do you remember the *Biddle grip*? It is how we hold the cards in the right hand in preparation for the overhand shuffle.

Hold them like that now, right fingers and thumb holding the deck by the short edges. Now turn the pack over with your left hand so the faces are showing. Now rotate the pack 90 degrees so you are holding it by the *long* edges, like in the picture.

Notice that the pack is NOT at the end of your fingers like it would be in an overhand shuffle. The edge of the deck is midway down your fingers, pressed against the middle phalanx (bone). This is why. Curl your fingers, closing them against the face of the pack (**pic 1**, below). Your index finger won't do much, but you need to press hard with the other three. Now draw these three fingers downward, and the face card will move with them. Your index finger helps keep the pack steady (**pic 2**). Turn your hand over, so the deck is face down. Practise gliding back the bottom card from this position (**pic 3**). This is how the glide will be performed mid-effect. The protruding card is invisible from the front, and hidden from above by your hand.

Pic 1	Pic 2	Pic 3

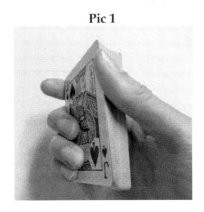 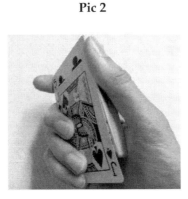 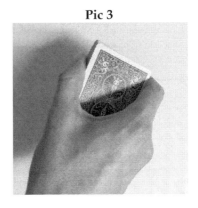

Notice in **pic 2** that the glided face card has exposed about a centimetre of that black 5. It is that 5 of clubs that you will draw out with your left hand, but the spectator thinks you draw out the face card, the jack of spades.

The glide takes some practise, but so does anything worth doing. Turn your right hand face down again and glide back the bottom card. Now bring your left hand, palm up, to the bottom of the deck. Touch your left fingertips to the exposed centimetre (the 5 of club in our example), which is the second card from bottom. Draw out this card with your fingertips, leaving the bottom card in place. Below is an exposed view. The jack of spades has been glided back by the right fingers, and the left fingertips are drawing out the 5 of clubs, which was second from bottom.

So in practise, you show the bottom card to the spectator (the jack of spades) turn your hand down and apparently draw it off the bottom of the pack. But what you really do is draw out the card above it, the five of clubs, leaving the bottom card in position.

Effect 7

<u>IMPOSSIBLE CARD CHANGE</u>

Effect: A card is chosen and signed. The deck is cut in two, and the signed card is put in one half of the pack. However, the magician produces the signed card from the *other* half, at any number the spectator chooses.

Method: I'm proud of this one. Have the deck freely shuffled and placed on the table. Ask a spectator to lift off roughly half the pack, and then to turn over the pile they hold and place it face up in front of them. They will have cut to a completely free selection. Let's say it's the five of clubs.

Using a permanent marker, get them to sign the face of the card. The card needn't be signed, but it's a nice addition because it proves their card is now one-of-a-kind.

Pick up the pile with their signed card on the face, after giving it a few moments to dry. Hold it in your right hand, face showing, in position for the glide. Turn your hand down, and glide off the card above it. The spectator thinks you hold their signed 5 of clubs in your left hand, when really you hold a random indifferent card.

Put the half pack you hold in your right hand face-down on the table. The other half is still in the middle of the table, and you bring the random card towards it. "I am going to put your signed card in *this* half of the deck," you say. Do NOT put it in the half you were just holding (the one with the chosen card still on the bottom). You put it in the other pile. Leave it sticking out halfway. Remember, everyone thinks it is the signed 5 of clubs.

"I need you to select one more card from *this* half," you say, picking up once more the pile nearest you, with the signed card on the bottom. Do NOT show the face of the pack you hold, for obvious reasons, but glide back the bottom card (the signed 5 of clubs) once more.

"Give me a number between 5 and 15."

Imagine they say *9*. You will draw out 8 cards from above the glided 5 of clubs and then take the *actual* 5 of clubs as the 9th card. Count out loud as you do this. If they say 13, you will glide out 12 random cards and take the actual 5 of clubs as the 13th. And so on. Keep every card face down as you do this.

Place the rest of the deck aside, and then put the signed 5 of clubs you hold face down in the middle of the table.

"Now, your signed card went in here…" Remember you left the fake 5 of clubs random card sticking out of that pile? Push it in now. "Then you selected the 9th (or 13th, or whatever) from *this* half. But, unbelievably, that card also happens to be… your signed card."

Turn it over. Bow.

Effect 8

THE WITCHES

Sometimes stories work well in magic. This is an interesting tale I made up with a surprise ending.

Effect: A tale of two sisters, accused of being witches, imprisoned for their imagined crimes. Except, they *were* witches after all.

Method: This effect requires a setup. First take out the two black queens and the two jokers. Now split the deck in half. Turn both piles over so they are face-up. Put each joker on the face of each pile. Then put each black queen on top of each joker. So you have two piles on the table, face-up, with the black queens showing, and jokers underneath them. This is how the effect begins.

Draw attention to the two piles, a black queen on each, and say, "Once upon a time there were two sisters. The queen of spades…" Pick up the pile with the queen of spades showing and hold it in position for the glide. "… and the queen of clubs." Gesture with your left hand to the other pile, still on the table. "Now, these sisters were accused of witchcraft by the other villagers, and they were put in two separate prisons."

We will assume there are at least two spectators (if there's only one, you can put the cards on the table instead of in their hands). Ask one spectator to hold out their hand, palm up.

"The queen of spades was put in the prison to the East…" Gesture to the pile in your right hand, which has the queen of spades showing. Now turn down your wrist and perform the glide. Draw out the joker and place it face-down on the spectator's open palm. Instruct them to put their other hand on top of it. Everyone will believe this is the queen of spades.

Put the pile you hold onto the table, keeping it face down. Remember, the queen of spades is still on the bottom.

Pick up the pile with the face up queen of clubs and ask another spectator to hold out their hand palm up. "And the queen of clubs was put in the prison to the West." Repeat the glide, drawing out the other joker and putting it face down on the spectator's empty palm. Get them to sandwich it with their other hand. You do NOT put down the pile you're holding.

"Now, the thing is – these sisters really *were* witches. And they had a magic number. It's a number between 1 and 10 – tell me what it is?"

A spectator gives a number. Let's say it's 5.

"5. Good." Glide back the queen of clubs, draw out four cards face down onto the table and take the queen as the fifth. Place the pile on top of the four cards you've just dealt. You still hold the queen of clubs face down in your left hand. Put it in the middle of the table now.

Pick up the other pile, with the queen of spades on the bottom. Glide out four cards and take the queen of spades as the fifth. Put it next to the other queen in the middle.

"You said 5. And actually, 5 *was* the magic number, because look – the queens have broken out of their prison cells."

Turn over the two queens. The spectators will find jokers in their own hands.

Alternative presentations:

1) Instead of jokers you can use the king and queen of diamonds. Change the story so that the King and Queen of the country put the two sisters into prison, and then at the end reveal that the witches swapped places with the King and Queen, having them put in prison in their place.

2) You can purchase blank face cards, if you desire. Use these blank cards in place of jokers so you can show that the prison cells were completely empty.

Effect 9

OUR CARD

Effect: This is a fun 'gotcha'. Two spectators pick cards, and then the magician picks one. The spectators are instructed to say the name of their cards at the same time – and are astonished when they say the *same* card! And then even more astonished when the card they said is actually in front of the magician!

Method: You need at least two spectators. If there are more, divide them into two groups. Have them stand at opposite ends of a table. You stand in the middle, one group on your right, the other on your left.

The deck can be freely shuffled by anyone. Put it on the table and have someone lift off about half the pack. Take it off them before anyone has seen the card they cut to, then discard the bottom half of the deck, which is still on the table.

You hold the top half. Get it in position for the glide, keeping it face down. Now turn to your right and show the face card to that group. Shield it from the others with your left hand. It's imperative the left group don't glimpse it.

"This is your card. Don't say the name of it out loud, I just want you all to remember it, okay?"

Then rotate your hand down, glide the face card back and draw out the card above it. Put it face down on the table. You won't know what either of those cards are, and that's okay. All you need to know is, the group has seen the face card and now think it's on the table in front of them. Really it's still on the bottom of the pack.

Now turn to the group to your left. The glided bottom card is still probably protruding a bit, so square the pack neatly together. Then show them the face card. It is the exact same card you just showed the other group, except they all think their card is on the table in front of them.

"This is your card. Please remember it."

Again, tilt your hand down, glide back the face card and draw out the one above it. Put it down on the table in front of the left hand group.

"And I will take a card for myself."

You will now take the *actual* bottom card and put it face down in front of you. You have shown this card to both groups, and both groups believe it is actually in front of them. They will not suspect they have seen the same card.

Discard the rest of the pack. Say, "Now, after three, I want everyone to say the name of the card they saw. 1, 2, 3…"

And of course both groups will say the *same* card. This will cause lots of amusement and surprise. They may even turn over the cards in front of them, causing more confusion on finding random cards.

Let's imagine both groups say the 5 of hearts. You say, "You both saw the 5 of hearts? Now, the *really* funny thing is that the 5 of hearts is *my* card." And you turn over the card in front of you, which will be the 5 of hearts.

SECTION THREE

THE BREAK

THE BREAK

The *break* is a very important and useful card sleight. In its own right, it holds the position of a card in a pack. It is also the basis for other sleights, such as false shuffles and forces, which you will come across later.

From the front, it looks like you're holding the deck of cards normally. But in the exposed view (see adjacent picture) you can see that the little finger is actually holding a gap in the pack, at a chosen position. This is called a break, and lets you keep track of a chosen card.

First, practise by holding the deck in your left hand in mechanic's grip. Now simply reach over with your right hand and take the deck by its short edges between your fingers and thumb. Lift up about half the deck from the back with your thumb, keeping the front of the pack flush. Insert the very tip of your left little finger into the gap, as in the above picture. Let go with your right hand, and the break should be maintained. It is only the *flesh* of your little finger that holds the break, NOT your fingernail, and it requires very little pressure. Keep practising until it feels natural.

CONTROLLING A SPECTATOR'S CARD

<u>Catching a break at a spectator's card</u>

First we need to catch a break above a spectator's chosen card. We'll start with an easier way and then learn a technique that is a bit trickier.

1) Spread the deck face down in both hands and have a spectator take out a card. Now square the pack as they look at it. Lift off about half the cards with your right hand, then gesture with your left hand to have the card replaced on that left hand packet.

Notice how your left fingers slightly protrude above the top of the packet. Bring the cards in your right hand down onto the left hand packet (the spectator's chosen card on top). As you do so, make sure your left little fingertip pokes into the gap and holds the break.

Practise lifting up half the pack and then replacing it, holding a break at the cut point. Make sure the cards are always flush from the front. When you can do this you are ready to jump to the next section, which involves bringing the chosen card to the top. You can head there now, or you can learn the alternative break control below.

2) Spread the deck face down in both hands and have a spectator take out a card as before. But instead of squaring the entire deck, now break the spread in two by lifting away your right hand.

Pic 1

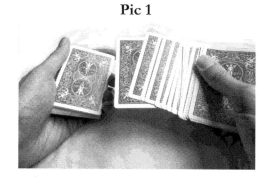

Square the cards in your left hand with your left fingers, and you'll be left in this position (**pic 1**). Gesture with your left hand and have the card returned on top of the left hand packet. Now the tricky bit. You need to bring your right hand back to your left, squaring the cards on top of the left hand packet – but you need to catch a *break*.

Do so thus: bring the right hand in at an angle, sloping down to the left. Push the right hand cards against your left thumb, beginning to square them. Your left fingers protrude above the left hand packet, meaning the cards from the right hand cannot lie flush on top of it.

Pic 2

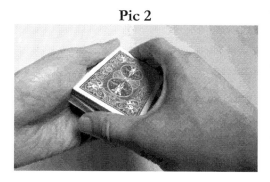

When the right hand cards are roughly on top of the left hand packet, resting on your left fingers, you need to readjust your right hand. Let go of the cards, and take them by the short edges between your fingers and thumb (**pic 2**). Now you can square the pack, being careful to keep your left little finger in the gap, keeping the break.

No matter which method you used, you are now holding a break above the spectator's chosen card. You are now ready to bring that card to the top.

Bring a chosen card to the top of the deck using the Cut To Table

You are holding a little finger break at the spectator's card. Not that they know this. If they do, you need to practise a bit more. The next step is to bring their card to the top of the deck, without them realizing that's what you've done.

So, the deck is secretly split in half at the little finger break. Look at the upper packet. Your right hand needs to lift off about half of that upper packet and then put it on the table. Then lift off the *rest* of that upper packet (now about half the size that it was) and put that on top of the cards on the table. Notice that your left hand now only holds the lower packet, with the spectator's chosen card on top.

Your right hand picks up the *whole* of that packet and puts it on top of the cards on the table, thus bringing the spectator's chosen card to the top.

<u>False shuffle, maintaining the top card in position</u>

You can add another convincer. Pick up the deck, chosen card on top. Now overhand shuffle, but instead of peeling off a small packet only peel off the top card in the first instance. Do so with your left thumb; simply slide the top card off into your left hand. Then shuffle the remaining cards on top.

Now the spectator's card is on the bottom of the deck. You need to shuffle it back to the top. Do so thus: overhand shuffle the majority of the pack until you're left with just half-a-dozen or so cards in your right hand (the spectator's card being one of them). Now peel off individual cards again with your left thumb. These last few cards go on top, one at a time. The last card is the spectator's card, and this will go down last, on the top of the deck.

Effect 10

<u>YOUR CARD AT YOUR NUMBER</u>

Effect: A card is selected then lost in the deck. A number is called. The chosen card is not at the number… or is it?

Method: Have a deck shuffled, and then spread the cards between your hands and have a spectator take out any card they wish. Have the card returned and bring it to the top using either of the methods mentioned previously.

Leave the cards on the table as you say, "I want you to think of a number between 5 and 20. Imagine you have psychic powers, and tell me the number that comes to you."

They say 15, for example.

"Great," you say. And you pick up the pack and begin dealing cards onto the table, counting out loud as you go. Notice that their chosen card will have gone down first (because you controlled it to the top of the deck) and now it is on the bottom of the dealt packet on the table.

You deal 14 cards into a pile, and then put the 15th card to one side. "Don't tell me what your card was," you say, picking up the packet of 14 cards and holding them in your right hand. "Just tell me, yes or no, whether that card is it." And tap the 15th card with the packet you hold.

Of course, it is not, because their card is at the face of the packet you hold. You must not flash it at them. But when you tap the 15th card, make sure you get a glimpse of it. It shouldn't be too difficult, because it is on the bottom of the packet. Just tilt your wrist down as you tap, exposing the face to you alone.

Say it's the jack of hearts. Remember it. Then put the 14-card packet back on top of the deck.

The spectator will turn over the 15th card, the one you tapped. It is not their card, of course, and they tell you, perhaps with sympathy, perhaps with glee.

"No worries," you say, and put the 15th card on top of the deck. "Not everyone has psychic powers, you understand. I do though – let me show you how it works…"

Hover your hand over the deck, as if you're sensing something. "I'm not getting a number… I'm actually getting the… jack of hearts…"

This will surprise them, as they will have no idea when you could have possibly seen their chosen card.

"And… you said you thought it was the 15th card, right?" Click your fingers over the deck. "Now. Count 15 cards and have a look."

Their chosen card is now, miraculously, number 15. Remember, dealing the 15 cards the first time reversed the order, so when you put the 14 card packet and then the initial 15th card on top of the deck it put their chosen card 15th from the top.

They deal 15 cards and are astonished when the jack of hearts is number 15.

Effect 11

<u>UNIVERSE</u>

There is a very famous card trick called *Out Of This World*. It is quite simple yet completely baffling, with many calling it the best card trick ever invented. It basically involves the spectator randomly dealing the deck into two separate piles. Afterwards, it is discovered that the pack has been perfectly separated into red cards and black cards.

The original required the magician to count the cards, and also to ask the spectator to reverse the colours halfway through. Paul Harris came up with a fabulous version called *Galaxy*, which required no card counting and no needless colour reversal. However, a suitably astute spectator might notice something amiss during the reveal (and have done, and have said so).

My version *does* require counting (sorry about that), but there's no colour reversal, and I believe the reveal is cleaner.

Effect: A deck of cards is given to a spectator, who deals them face down, randomly, into two piles. Afterwards, it is discovered that the pack has been perfectly separated into red cards and black cards.

Method: The setup is exactly the same as for *Out Of This World* and its other variations. You need to start with the pack already separated into red and black. Have the 26 black cards on the bottom and the 26 red cards making up the top half of the deck.

It is possible to false shuffle the deck in front of the spectator beforehand, although it isn't essential. An overhand shuffle would really mess things up, though! You need to do a standard riffle shuffle (but be prepared to clean up). You can skip the following section and perform this effect without a shuffle, but for an added convincer the details are below.

Shuffling whilst maintaining the setup:

By apparently shuffling the deck, you convince the spectator that the order of the cards is completely random (when of course it is not). The easiest method is the standard riffle shuffle. Take the deck (don't worry about the setup for now; we're only practising) and cut it in half.

Pick up both piles by their short edges as in **pic 1** below. Notice that your index fingers are on top. Now bend each half as in **pic 2**, pushing in with your index fingers and pulling up with your thumbs. Now let cards fall (riffle) off your thumbs by moving them across the beveled edge of the packets (**pic 3**). Let the cards interlink as they fall from either hand. This doesn't need to be perfect! You don't need to link single card by single card. Small packets of two or three cards will fall, and that is fine. The more you practise the smoother your riffle shuffle will become.

Pic 1	Pic 2	Pic 3

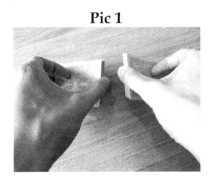 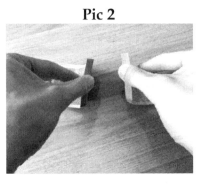 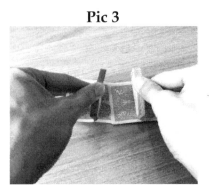

Now, back to the trick. You can use the riffle shuffle to make it look like the cards are thoroughly mixed, when in fact you have the deck separated by colour. You need to have the deck setup slightly differently. You need two separate piles. Each pile consists of 13 black cards on the bottom and 13 red cards on top.

When you riffle shuffle them together, the bottom black cards of both piles will weave together, and the upper red cards will weave together. You will end up with the deck roughly separated, red on black. HOWEVER, there will be a few out of place cards in the middle (how many depends on your riffle shuffle! The better the shuffle the fewer out of place cards). If you're feeling really brave you can even slide both piles across the table to the spectator for them to riffle shuffle together.

After the shuffle say, "I want you to concentrate on a few cards. I'm going to pick them out now." And you need to pick out all the out of place red cards that are in the black section. They will be dotted about in the middle of the pack. Pick them all out and put them face down on the table until you've got them all. The pack should be perfectly separated now, red cards to the left, black cards to the right.

Table the deck and pick up the red cards you withdrew. Hold them up, the backs to the spectator. "Really think about it. What colour do you think these are?"

If they say red, okay, you tell them they should be good at this. If they say black, tell them it's okay, they got it wrong, but not to worry. You'll see what happens when their subconscious takes control, when they *don't* think about it. Put the red cards you're holding in the middle of the red section of the deck. You are now ready to begin. The deck has been shuffled, but is perfectly separated, red on black.

The workings:

Tell the spectator that the deck is made up of red cards and black cards, and hand them the pack. "The cards are to remain face-down throughout. I want you to deal the cards, one at a time – if you think the card is red, put it on the table and make a pile. If you think it's black, give it to me. Okay? Don't think about it too hard. Begin when you like."

The spectator will start dealing from the top of the deck, either into a pile on the table, or passing them to you. When a card is handed to you, take it with your right hand and put it in your left palm in mechanic's grip. Remember, the top cards are all red, and you need to count them all, because you need to know when the spectator starts handing out black cards. So secretly count in your head the 26 red cards. Remember to count the ones that go on the table too, not just the ones that go in your hand! The 27th card onward will all be black.

Now, the 27th (first black) card might go down on the table or it might be passed to you. It doesn't matter. All you need to remember is that after you've counted 26, the next card the spectator passes to you will be black. It could be the 27th card, it could be the 30th, 31st, 34th, whatever. But it will be black. When you take that card you will catch a little finger break under it when you put it into your left hand. There is no need to continue counting. Take the rest of the black cards the spectator passes and put them onto the pile in your left, maintaining the break.

Eventually the spectator will have dealt all the cards. There will be a pile in front of them, black cards on red cards. And then there's the pile in your left hand, also black cards on top, red cards underneath, but you have a break between the colours.

"You separated the pack into two piles," you say. With your right hand adjust the pile in your left hand. Lift up the upper half into a wide mouth, but keep the front edge flush like the opposite picture. Hold the gap in place with your left fingers. The bottom packet is all red, the upper packet is all black. The spectator should not know the large gap exists.

Pick up the pile in front of the spectator. "You thought these were all red cards. And you gave me the cards you thought were black. Look what's happened."

You're going to make it look like you put the cards in your left hand on top of the pile in your right hand. But what you really do is put the cards in your right hand *in the mouth*, in the gap in the left hand pile. i.e. *Between* the separated red and black cards. This puts the black cards with the black cards and the red cards with the red cards.

Turn the whole thing over and spread the deck, showing how perfectly they've been separated.

Effect 12

<u>ULTIMATE SNAP</u>

This idea came to me from a Paul Harris effect, where a spectator and a magician play *snap* – they try to be the first to slap their hand down on a spectator's card. The spectator wins, however it's discovered they've slapped the wrong card. It's a classic gotcha. My version doesn't require a force (more on forces later) and has another surprise ending.

Effect: A spectator chooses a card. The magician writes down a prediction. They then play *snap*, both trying to slap their hand down on the card first. The spectator wins. "Ah," says the magician. "I thought it was a different card. Read what I wrote." On the paper the magician has indeed written the wrong card. However, he then produces the spectator's card from his pocket, and the spectator turns over the card they slapped to find it matches the prediction.

Method: Firstly, have the spectator choose a card and remember it. Then take it back and control it to the top with the break and cut to table. Now overhand shuffle the card to the bottom and then back to the top as an added convincer.

Give the deck to the spectator and ask them to deal between 15 and 20 cards, one-by-one, into a pile onto the table. They do so. Move the rest of the deck aside and then pick up the pile of dealt cards. The spectator's chosen card will be at the bottom of the packet (because it was the top card, and they dealt it down first). Do not let the spectator see it!

Look at the face card of the packet, which is the spectator's chosen card. Say it's the 9 of diamonds. Remember it. Now spread the cards between your hands, in front of your face, the backs showing to the spectator. With your left thumb slide the 9 of diamonds to the left, off the face of the pile. It needs to come towards the middle of the spread, so the spectator won't notice it was on the face. In the same motion, spread the cards face-up on the table, in a grid, in a rough square with little overlap.

"Do you see your card?" you ask. The spectator says yes. "Oh good," you continue, "we can use these then."

With both hands, divide the grid in two, sweeping the cards apart into two separate groups. "Which group has your card?" you ask.

The spectator points to the group with the 9 of diamonds in it. Sweep the other group up and put it on top of the deck out of the way. Now gather the group with the spectator's card in it and give it to the spectator to shuffle.

They shuffle the pile and hand it back to you. "Okay, I'm going to look through the cards and make a prediction," you say. Look through the pile and locate the 9 of diamonds. It needs to be somewhere in the middle. If it's not, no big deal, just move it there. Now look at the card directly behind the 9 of diamonds (to its left). Say it's the ace of clubs. *This card* will be your prediction, and will be the card the spectator ends up slapping.

Put the packet face down and write *ace of clubs* secretly on some paper. Fold it up and set it in front of the spectator. Pick up the packet again. "We're going to play snap," you say. "I'm going to show you the cards in this pile and then place them onto the tabletop. When you see your card go down, you need to slap your hand on top of it. I'm going to try to anticipate your card and beat you to it." You're not, of course, but this adds drama.

Put the packet in your right hand in position for the glide (aha, you're thinking now). The face card needs to be showing. Say its name. It's any random card. Turn your wrist down and slide out that actual card. Put it face down in the middle of the table.

"So, if that had been your card you would slap your hand on top of it," you explain for anyone in the crowd who's a bit slow. "Got it?"

Move that card aside so the middle of the table is clear. Show the face of the packet again. Say the card's name. Tilt your wrist down and slide out that actual card, exactly as before. Put it face-down, and kind of jerk your left hand a bit as you let it go, as if you were thinking about slapping it. You joker, you. "Ooh, I thought that might have been it."

It remains unslapped, so move it aside with the other.

Repeat with the other random cards, dropping them down and then moving them aside. Eventually you will be showing the face of the 9 of diamonds. Maybe a stir will go round the room. "9 of diamonds," you say. Tilt your wrist and perform the glide. Draw out the card above it, which will of course be the ace of clubs.

Drop it face down, and the spectator slaps it. Look bewildered. If they look like they're going to turn it over in the glory of their success, stop them. "It was the *9 of diamonds?*" you say. "I really didn't think it was that one! Okay. Just leave the card in the middle of the table. Now, open the paper and read out what I wrote at the beginning."

As all eyes turn to the paper-opener, simply put the cards you're holding in your right hand into your jacket (or coat) pocket. Don't look at what you're doing, but you need to know whether the bottom card (the 9 of diamonds) is facing out or facing in against your body. Unless you flip the packet over (and why would you do that?) it should be facing in against your body, with the back of the top card facing out to the right. It doesn't even matter if anyone sees you do this. All you're doing is getting rid of the cards, putting them away. Read the alternative presentations at the end for other ideas.

So someone opens the paper and sees you actually wrote *ace of clubs* on it. "Oh!" you say. "So I didn't write the 9 of diamonds!"

The spectators start laughing at how badly the trick is going.

"But that's okay," you continue. "Because *that's* not the 9 of diamonds either," and you point to the card face down on the table. "Because the 9 of diamonds is in my pocket." Stand up and openly put your empty right hand into your right pocket and draw out the bottom card from the packet.

Put the 9 of diamonds face up on the table. This causes quite a reaction. Someone will probably turn over the card on the table and find that it's the ace of clubs. If not, tell them to. "So my prediction *was* correct! You *did* slap the ace of clubs!"

Alternative presentations

If you're standing round a table, putting it into a jacket pocket is the best idea. If you're **sitting** at the table, you can try this. When someone is opening the folded paper, bring the packet you're holding with your right hand in front of you. It is still held face down, in glide position. Hold the packet's left short edge with your left hand too. Rest your hands on the edge of the table. Now press your right fingers against the bottom card (the 9 of diamonds) and push them towards you. The bottom card will slide towards you. Let it fall right into your lap, unnoticed by everyone else. Put the packet down and put your hands in your lap.

Now, whilst everyone's eyes are averted, you can take the 9 of diamonds and put it in a trouser pocket. Or – and this would be my preference – roll up your left trouser leg and put it in your *sock*. Let your trouser leg fall back into place. This is an idea from one of Derren Brown's card routines. That makes for an interesting reveal!

SECTION FOUR

BASIC COIN HANDLING

COIN MAGIC

Coin magic is also very popular. There are always coins lying about, waiting to be picked up and vanished and used to mystify. There are different types of vanishes, and we will look at three: the French drop; the classic palm vanish; and my own retention vanish. Eventually, we can put them all together into routines, which you'll find in section nine.

When it comes to handling coins and performing sleights and palms, the bigger the coin is usually the better. In the UK, a 2p piece is the perfect size. A 10p is also useful, but perhaps less so. A 50p is large but I don't like it because it's not round. Other coins are generally too small, but that might just be because I have big hands.

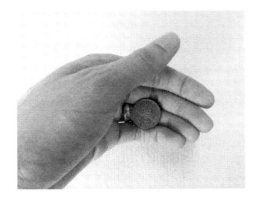

We must first get used to the *finger palm*. Have a look at the opposite picture. Yes. It's just holding the coin in your naturally curled fingers. Practise with both your hands, letting the coin rest against your fingers. You don't need to close them against the coin; just relax your hand and your fingers will curl naturally – but keep them together! Keep your arm and hand movements natural.

Holding coins in both hands in finger palm, practise keeping your arms at your side, whilst standing, whilst sitting, whilst leaning over a table. Move your arms, and your hands, keeping everything natural, without stiffness.

Effect 13

TWO VANISHES

The French Drop

"Le Tourniquet" in French. This is one of the oldest methods for vanishing coins, dating back hundreds of years. Hold the coin in your left hand as in **pic 1** on the next page. Your hand is palm up. The coin is held by its edge between the fingers and thumb, and faces upwards. Reach over with your right hand in a pincer

motion, fingers on top, thumb underneath (**pic 2**). Pretend to grasp the coin between your thumb and fingers. What you actually do is let the coin fall unseen into your left hand (**pic 3**).

Pic 1   Pic 2   Pic 3

  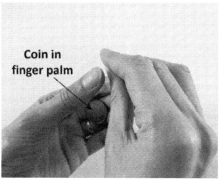

Lift your right hand as if holding the coin. Your left hand drops naturally to your side, the coin now held secretly in finger palm. Bring your right hand up to eye level, so the spectator is looking at the back of your fingers and you are looking at the back of your thumb. Rub your thumb against your fingers. Slowly tilt your hand and open your fingers to show that the coin has vanished.

This sleight can be performed standing or sitting. It is very effective when performed well, so make sure you practise it lots and lots in front of a mirror. You need to make the 'taking of the coin' and the dropping of your left hand to your side completely natural and fluent, so it become second nature. The left hand falling and the right hand lifting up should happen at the same instant.

After the vanish, the question is what to do with the coin hidden in your left hand. There are a few options. The classic presentation (and this works especially well on small children) is to now reproduce the coin from behind a spectator's ear. Quickly reach out your left hand to an unsuspecting ear, pushing the coin to the tips of your fingers with your thumb. Then draw your hand back into view slowly, holding the coin at your fingertips.

The other option is to ditch the coin, either afterwards or during. If you're standing: When you supposedly take the coin in your right hand, you can tilt your body slightly, bringing your right foot forward, which takes your left arm out of view behind you. And simply ditch it in a pocket when the spectator's concentration is on your right hand.

Or afterwards, you can put your left hand into your pocket to get out a pack of cards to do another trick! And obviously ditch the coin as you do so. Or at the start of the trick have a few coins lying on a table. Pick up one of them and perform the French drop. Afterwards, scoop up the coins again with your left hand, depositing the palmed coin in with them.

If you're sitting: It's a little easier. After supposedly taking the coin in your right hand, simply rest your left hand on the table, the backs of your fingers to the spectators, and when all eyes are on your held up right hand, drop the coin into your lap. This allows you to do a completely clean, both hands empty vanish. Make sure you *do* show both hands empty at the end, because you can.

If you are sitting but not at a table, drop your left hand to the seat of the chair, next to your left leg. Secretly push the coin under your left thigh whilst the spectator is distracted, looking at your upheld right hand. Again, you can show both hands empty.

If your hands are empty, instead of rubbing your right fingers with your thumb, try this instead: take your left hand to your right hand, fingertips to fingertips, as if you're holding the coin with both sets of fingers and thumbs. Lock your left index fingernail under your right thumbnail, as in the opposite picture. Now *click* the two together as you break your hands apart. It will look and sound as if you have snapped the coin in two!

Matt Walker's Retention Vanish

There are different variations of the retention vanish, but the concept is the same: the spectator *sees* the coin go into one hand, when really it is retained in the other. This is mine. I'm going to level with you: I don't much like it. When I vanish a coin I use either the French drop or the classic palm vanish (next up). I feel about this little creation of mine the same way you'd feel if you had a child but didn't like it because other people's kids are better. Anyway. You might find it useful, eh?

Hold the coin in your right hand, between your thumb and first two fingers, as in the opposite picture. Your left hand is held palm up close by. You will bring your right hand to your left and apparently enclose it in your left hand. Actually, you hit the edge of the coin firmly against the fleshy heel of your left thumb (marked **X** in the picture) and release it at the same moment. It is propelled back into your right hand into finger palm position.

Your left fingers come up and over as you do this, hiding the mechanics and the empty left palm. As soon as the coin has rebounded into finger palm, you withdraw your right hand and close your left fingers, making a fist. The illusion is completed by extending your right index finger as you bring your right hand back, having closed your left fingers around it.

THE CLASSIC PALM

The classic palm is a very useful sleight and worth the effort to master. It can be used as a vanish in and of itself, and also as a switch and retention in other tricks and routines. Here is how it works. The coin is held in the right palm, trapped between the fleshy heel of the thumb and the flesh beneath the fourth and fifth finger.

Look at the opposite picture. In this position, the hand can be turned over, held completely natural, the fingers can move, and the coin will stay in position. Practise like this: place the coin in the middle of your right palm. Now bring your thumb and little finger together, so their tips touch. See what happens to the coin? It gets trapped between the flesh of your palm.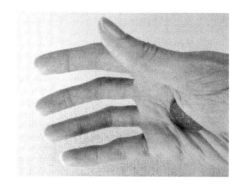

Keep your thumb and little finger touching and turn your hand over. It will look like you're making a weird shadow puppet. The coin will also stay in your palm. Now, keep your thumb in that position but move your little finger away. *This* is the classic palm. Notice how it looks and feels. Practise putting the coin in your hand and 'pinching' it into palm position, but this time don't go so far as touching your thumb to your little fingertip. See how you can still wiggle your fingers and move your hand naturally with the coin classic palmed. In fact, I wrote this paragraph with a 2p classic palmed, if you care.

TRICKS WITH THE CLASSIC PALM

Effect 14

THE CLASSIC PALM VANISH

Place the coin into the palm of your right hand, in position for the classic palm. Turn your left hand palm up, showing it empty. Now tip over your right hand, on top of your left palm, as if tipping the coin into it. Instead, keep the coin palmed in your right hand. As you withdraw your right hand, bring your left fingers up and close them so you make a fist.

The spectators will think the coin is held in your left fist when in reality it is classic palmed in your right hand. Remember to act natural at all times with your right hand and arm. Drop it to your side if you are standing. If you are sitting at a table, simply move your hand to the edge of the table top and drop the coin into your lap.

You can dispose of the coin in any of the ways mentioned previously. Lapping remains the best method, but obviously is only possible if you're sitting at a table. The advantage of having a coin classic palmed rather than finger palmed, is that you can still use your hand for most purposes and the spectator will never know. You can pick up spare coins on the table, get something out of your pocket, even *write* with a coin classic palmed. And it is a simple matter of releasing the coin and catching it in finger palm if you wish to reproduce it from behind an ear.

Effect 15

COIN TO SMALL OBJECT

TRANSFORMATION

Mechanically, the method is exactly the same as the previous vanish. You apparently tip the coin into your left hand but retain it in classic palm in your right. But this time you need a small object *already hidden in your left hand*. It could be a paper clip, a rubber, a button… or maybe a different coin, like a 10p. Obviously, you cannot show your left hand empty, because it is *not* empty. So you will need to keep your fingers slightly curled to hide the object.

Try not to draw attention to your left hand at all. Make sure all eyes are on the 2p lying on your right palm. Quickly, turn it over your left, cupping them together, palming the coin. Then remove your right hand as you close your left into a fist. Open your left hand, revealing the coin has changed into another small object.

You could present it as a simple feat of mentalism. Find a 2p and look at the face that has the Queen's head. This side has the year it was minted. Write that year on a bit of paper and put it in a pocket. Now, secretly finger palm that coin in your left hand and go find some suitable spectators. Ask them to bring out any change. Make sure they have a 2p that looks similar to the one you have palmed. No good picking a bright shiny one if yours is old and dull. If they don't have a suitable coin, or no 2p at all (maybe they only carry notes), run away.

Okay. So you've spied the suitable 2p. Bring out the paper and hand it someone. Then take the spectator's 2p with your right hand, drop it onto your palm and shimmy it into position. If you need to prod it with your left index finger, that's okay. Just make sure that your secret coin is hidden.

Apparently drop their coin into your left hand. What you really do, of course, is palm their coin as you tip your right hand over. The coin in your left hand is the one you prepared earlier. Draw attention to the date. It's the date you predicted.

Effect 16

<u>COIN THROUGH GLASS</u>

You need a small glass tumbler and a 2p coin. Have the coin signed by a spectator with their initials, or two random letters, or a number if you prefer. You'll need a permanent marker, not a pencil, obvs. Take the coin on your right palm and classic palm it when you pretend to drop it into your left. Keep your left fingers curled up, hiding your palm, but this time *do not close it into a fist.*

Keeping the coin classic palmed in your right hand, pick up the glass by the rim. Make sure the coin is directly over the hole. Slap the bottom of the glass against your left palm and release the coin from your right at the same moment.

It will make a lovely tinkling sound. A slight up-down motion with your left hand as you cup the bottom of the glass may enhance the illusion. Hold up the glass, showing the coin has passed through.

SECTION FIVE

CARD FORCES

A card force is almost self-explanatory. You *force* a spectator to choose the card you want them to pick, whilst apparently giving them a free choice. There are many ways of doing forces. We will learn the easiest one (the cross cut force), the best one (the riffle force), and the most natural (the classic force, although this one doesn't always work). Then we'll learn various effects and presentations.

The Cross Cut Force

The card you wish to force (the *force card*) is on top of the deck. Say it's the seven of hearts. You can show the spectator that all the cards are different, but avoid showing the top card (the one furthest to your left when you spread) as this is the card you will force on them.

Place the deck on the table in front of them and ask them to cut the deck anywhere they like. If they look confused, ask them to simply pick up a block of cards from the top of the deck. It doesn't matter how many cards they pick up. Ask them to place their packet on the table next to the remaining cards.

Say the packet they picked up is **A**. The force card is on top of **A**. The lower packet left on the table is **B**. They placed **A** next to **B** at your direction. Now, pick up the lower packet **B** and place it on top of **A**, at 90 degrees as in the picture. Notice where the force card is: at the top of packet **A**.

Now you need to take a few moments explaining what is to come. Ask them if they believe in psychic abilities, or if they've ever heard of people who can read minds. What you say depends a lot on the effect you are about to perform – but what you want to do is distract them from the cards for a moment. Take their mind off what has just happened. You want them to forget what you did with the deck.

After their distraction, bring them back to the deck. "You cut the pack wherever you wanted," you say, and lift packet **B** off packet **A** and set it aside. "Have a look at the card you cut to." And touch the top card of packet **A**, which is the force card. They will believe it is the card they cut to, when it's actually the card that was on top of the deck to begin with.

The Riffle Force

The riffle force is my favourite force, and many other magicians' favourite force too. It is easy to see why. It is failsafe and convincing and natural. The first thing to practise is riffling the cards.

Hold the deck in mechanic's grip in your left hand. Now move your left thumb off the edge of the deck and put it on top, in the middle of the top card. Bring your right hand over and on top of the deck, thumb at the back, fingers at the front. Put your right index finger to the front left corner of the deck, but reaching over so it presses against the edge of the deck, all 52 cards, as in the picture.

Press in your right index finger and slightly lift it, putting pressure on the deck, which will bend upwards. Now release each card in turn, starting from the bottom card, by running your finger up the corner edge of the deck.

It will make a distinctive ripping sound and, if you hold it to your face, will give you a nice breeze.

That is the riffle. Now we need the 'force' bit. That involves catching a break above the force card, and the best way to do that is the *swing cut.*

The swing cut

The swing cut is a useful flourish, allowing you to cut the deck in your hands. Hold the deck in your left hand in mechanic's grip. With your right hand, pinch the deck with your thumb at the back and two fingers at the front right corner (**pic 1**). Now take the weight of the deck in your right hand. This next step will take a little work. Press your two right fingers (index and middle) firmly into the deck. Now split them, lifting your index finger. With practise, the deck will split in two, as in **pic 2**.

Take the top packet in the crook of your left thumb as in **pic 3**. Release your right index finger and move your left hand away, holding the top packet tight in the crook of the thumb. The lower packet in your right hand comes over the left hand packet and you drop it on top. You have now cut the deck in your hands.

Pic 1	**Pic 2**	**Pic 3**
	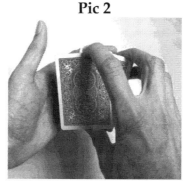	

When performing the riffle force, you want the force card on top of the deck again. Now swing cut the top half and take it in your left hand. When you bring the right hand packet down, catch a little finger break below it. This will leave you with the deck in mechanic's grip in your left hand, with the force card in the middle and a break above it. If you lift all the cards above the break off, the top card in your left hand will be the force card. Makes sense? Good.

So, you have a break above the force card. Say to the spectator, "Just tell me when to stop." (Saying 'stop' is a surefire clue that a force is being committed). You now riffle the front corner of the deck with your right index finger, *keeping the break*. The spectator says 'stop' and you stop immediately, mid-riffle, holding open the front of the deck with your right index finger, and secretly holding open the back of the deck with your left pinky.

Now, you are apparently going to cut the deck where the spectator stopped you. But that is not what happens. Have you guessed it? You actually lift off all the cards *above the break*. Your right thumb takes the lead here. You actually lift the back of the cards first, your right thumb lifting all the cards above the break. Your right index finger just plays along. Your 3rd, 4th, and 5th right fingers are the ones to actually pincer the upper packet with your thumb.

You lift away the upper packet and hold out the lower packet, saying, "Take a look at that card." It is, of course, the force card.

The Classic Force

This is a beautiful force… when it works. As I mentioned previously, 'say stop' is a sure signpost to a magician's force. The trouble can come when you've been constantly asking a spectator to pick a card by spreading the cards in your hand, and then suddenly you change it to "Say stop." It can seem fishy. Of course, you could make every selection, including free choices, a *just say stop* selection. That, dear reader, is up to you.

Otherwise, try this. Have the force card on top. Swing cut the deck and catch a break. Apologies for the déjà vu. Now ask the spectator to hold out a finger. Begin spreading the cards below their finger as you say, "I want you to just touch the back of one of these cards."

Spreading the cards from your left hand to your right whilst holding the break is a strange sensation. You need to press your left pinky firmly up against the deck to keep the break in place. But it is possible, and you *can* feel when you're coming to the break in your spread. The card just above the break will end up stuck to the pad of your left little finger. The next card (the one under it, to its left) is the force card.

You need to time the spread perfectly. When you get to the force card lift it subtly towards the spectator's finger. Hopefully they'll touch it.

And that's all there is to it. It works maybe 80% of the time. Seriously. If it doesn't work and they touch another card, well that's fine too. Just do another trick that doesn't require a force.

Effect 17

<u>PICTURE YOUR CARD</u>

It's no good simply forcing a card and telling the spectator what the card is... or is it? This effect does exactly that, but using showmanship, and makes it look like you are using subtle cues from the spectator to deduce the name of their card. In actuality, of course, you know their card from the start, because you have force it on them.

Force a picture card. A king, queen or jack. Say the jack of clubs. Why does it have to be a picture card? You'll see in a moment. Have the spectator remember it and then lose it back into the deck.

"I'm going to ask you some questions," you say, "and I want you to answer, but in your head. Don't say anything out loud. Understand?"

If they don't, try asking in French.

"First, can you picture your card?" Regardless of how they react, you say, "Hmmm, you seemed to take a while to do that – which might mean it's quite difficult to imagine. Does that mean it's a picture card? No, don't say anything!"

They will invariably be smiling at your deductive prowess.

"Okay, so it's a picture card. Now to work out what the suit is." Say, "Hearts, diamonds, spades, clubs," over and over again. Slow down on the *spades, clubs* – pretend to get subtle clues from their expression. You put a bit more emphasis on *spades*, and then say, "No! It's clubs isn't it!"

Or, whilst you're repeating the names of the suits, take their wrist and pretend to take their pulse. "Your pulse gets quicker when I call out the correct suit. You can't help it." A load of baloney, of course. But you settle on clubs and all are amazed.

"Okay, so it's a picture card club. Can you now say to me 'jack, queen, king, ace' – say them out loud, over and over."

You get the spectator to say *jack, queen, king, ace,* and you pretend their voice wobbles a little on *jack*. After a moment you proclaim: "It's the jack of clubs, isn't it!" and all gasp in wonder.

Effect 18

<u>GO SOIL YOURSELF</u>

Effect: You're outside, in a garden. Perhaps you're on a picnic. "Oh look, a deck of cards," you say. The spectator picks one. You take some soil from the ground and rub it on your arm. The name of the chosen card magically appears there, writ in soil.

Method: No, you don't try to write the card name on your arm whilst you rub it, that would fool no one. You need to prepare your arm beforehand with a secret ingredient: soap. You also need dry soil to hand. A flower bed is perfect. It cannot be wet, okay? This is no rainy day trick.

First, you need a force card on top of the deck. The 7 of hearts works perfectly, as it's all straight lines. Curves are harder. Say you need a wee or a poo, if you wish, and go to the toilet. Go, if the urge takes you. Now you need a bar of soap. I don't know if squirty soap works. Perhaps you can try it and let me know. Anyway, wet the soap bar under the tap, then scrub your finger in it. Turn your left arm palm up and write **7H** on the underside of your forearm, in soap.

Go outside. Force the 7 of hearts. Say, "Really concentrate on your card. Now watch." Take a handful of dry soil in your fingers and rub it on your forearm. The soil will stick to the soap, and **7H** will appear on your arm in dirt residue.

Effect 19

<u>WIPE YOUR GLASS</u>

What better way to follow *Go Soil Yourself*?

Effect: This startling effect involves Merlin (the jack of spades) magically revealing a spectator's chosen card. You show a clear plastic sheet with the jack of spades drawn on it in marker. "This is Merlin," you explain. I don't know why. The spectator picks a card. You wave your hand over the plastic sheet and the jack of spades drawn on it magically changes to their chosen card.

Method: Obviously, this trick requires a setup. You need something flat and see-through to draw on. Preferably glass or plastic. You can buy A4 sheets of clear plastic. Food packaging often has a plastic window you can remove from the cardboard. That works fine. Or you could use a clear plastic box, or a glass chopping board (gulp) or even a *window*. PLEASE FOR THE LOVE OF GOD USE A WASHABLE PEN. DO NOT USE A PERMANENT MARKER OH MY GOD

Let's imagine you have a sheet of clear plastic acetate. You need to draw the force card, which is going to be the 7 of clubs, as a *mirror image*, for reasons explained later. The picture opposite shows you what you need to draw. If you are using disposable acetate, you can draw this in permanent marker for repeated use. *If you are drawing on anything else <u>NON-DISPOSABLE</u>* like a window or a glass table then you MUST use a washable pen!

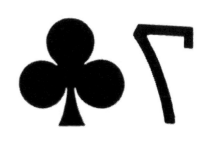

I'm sorry to shout but I don't want any angry letters from your parents or your wives. Make sure you can rub off the marker you're using with your hand.

When the mirrored 7 of clubs is drawn, turn the plastic over. You will see it written the right way round. You are now going to draw the jack of spades *over* the 7 of clubs, on this side of the plastic. You will understand why I have chosen the 7 of clubs as the force card. You can turn the 7 into a J by extending the lines. And you can turn the clubs into a spade by drawing a triangle over the 3 cauliflower bumps.

Now, if you rub your hand over the sheet, you rub away the jack of spades and reveal the 7 of clubs from the other side of the plastic.

So. You need the plastic or glass prepared, with both cards drawn on. Take out the jack of spades from the pack and put the 7 of clubs on top. Draw attention to the jack of spades card and say, "This is Merlin. He's a wizard. You may have heard of him." I guess you could call him Harry Potter if you really wish. "Merlin has drawn his self portrait here – isn't it good?"

Draw attention to the plastic, which you can hold up. "Yes, it's beautiful. I need you to choose a card now."

Force the 7 of clubs on the spectator and ask them to remember it. "Now, because Merlin/Harry is a wizard, he can tell me what your card is. Watch." Rub your hand over the plastic, erasing the written jack of spades, which changes into the name of their card, the seven of clubs.

Alternative presentation: If you find the clubs symbol too difficult to draw (and there's no shame in that), simply write **7c** and turn it into **Js**. The **c** can become an **s** quite easily, by extending the curl downwards and around to the left.

Effect 20

<u>SIBLINGS</u>

This is my variation on the earlier *TWINS*. It is even more magical.

Effect: Two cards are chosen by a spectator and then dealt back into the deck face-up, at positions of their choosing. These cards magically locate their siblings.

Method: You need two pairs of *siblings* – two cards that share the same colour and number, i.e. the 5 of clubs and the 5 of spades, which are both black 5s. Let us use the black 5s (five of spades and clubs) and the red 10s (ten of hearts and diamonds). Remove them from the deck. Now take the 5 of spades and put it on the bottom of the deck. Put the 10 of hearts on top. Now put the 5 of clubs and the 10 of diamonds on top of that, in any order.

You are ready to begin. Swing cut the deck and catch a break, and then perform the riffle force. Offer the packet in your left hand, which the spectator will believe they stopped you at. It is the original top of the deck. Ask them to remove two cards, which are the 10 of diamonds and the 5 of clubs.

They do so. Now put the left hand packet back on top of the right hand packet. This keeps the bottom card as the 5 of spades and the 10 of hearts on top.

The spectator holds the 5 of clubs and 10 of diamonds. Put the deck on the table and take the two cards from the spectator. "It's okay for us all to see what they are." Place them face up on the table.

You will now perform *Twins* with these cards. Begin dealing the deck into a pile, and ask the spectator to say stop when they wish. They do so. You put the 5 clubs face up on the dealt pile. Then put the remainder of the deck on top of that, squashing the two black 5s together.

Repeat that step, dealing a pile until the spectator says stop. Put the 10 of diamonds face up on top of the dealt pile. Then when you drop the rest of the cards on top, it'll put the two red 10s face to face.

Spread the entire pack on the table, and point to the two 'chosen' (forced) cards, which are face up in the spread. With two fingers, pull out the 5 of clubs and the face down card lying directly on top of it, which will be the 5 of spades. Repeat with the 10 of diamonds and the card lying face down on top of it (the 10 of hearts). Reveal that those chosen cards have found their twins.

Effect 21

<u>YOU LOOK LOVELY IN RED</u>

This has two reveals, the second even better than the first.

Effect: You leave a scrunched up bit of paper on the table. The spectator chooses a card from a blue-backed deck. It is the 8 of spades. A spectator opens the paper. *8 of spades*, it says. And also: *RED*. But the 8 of spades isn't red! You turn the card over. The *back* is red, and it's the only red-backed card in the deck.

Method: You need a deck of any colour and a single card of any different colour. We'll assume a blue-backed deck and a red-backed card. Say the red-backed card is the 8 of spades. Have this card on the bottom of the blue-backed deck, and put it in a blue card box.

Write '8 of spades' in large letters on a piece of paper, and then RED in one corner, upside down, so it's legible but easily overlooked. Screw up the paper and leave it in the middle of the table.

Ask a spectator to pass you the card box and take out the cards. "We're going to use a pack of cards," you say, and casually spread them face-down in your hands. Do not flash the red back at the bottom, and close the spread after a second or two. The spectator will notice that they are 'all' blue-backed.

Perform the swing cut and catch a break below the red-backed 8 of spades. Ask the spectator to stop as you perform the riffle force. This time however, when you lift off all the cards above the break in your right hand, you do *not* offer the left hand lower packet. Instead, you turn over the packet in your right hand, palm up, exposing the 8 of spades.

Put the packet in your left hand on the table. Peel off the 8 of spades from the packet in your right hand. Place it face up next to the screwed up ball of paper. Do *not* flash the back. The spectator assumes it is blue-backed, like all the others.

Discard the rest of the pack. Say, "I made a prediction – can you open the paper and tell everyone what's written?"

The spectator reads, "8 of spades," and hopefully this gets a reaction.

"Is there anything else written on the paper?"

"Yes." The spectator squints. Puts on their glasses. Asks for a microscope. "It says *red*."

"Mmmm," you say. "The 8 of spades is a black card, not a red card… but wait…" You turn the card over, exposing the red back. "You managed to pick the only red card in the entire blue deck."

Effect 22

DREAM CARD

Daryl's *Dream Card* is one of the greatest pieces of card magic you are ever likely to see. This is my version, which doesn't need a double-backed card, gimmicked wallet, triple lift or tricky two-card top palm.

Effect: You have a red-backed deck of cards and an envelope on the table. You withdraw a card from the envelope, showing only the back, which is blue. Your signature is on the back, and you say this card came to you in a dream. You slide the card back into the envelope and get a spectator to pick a card from the red-backed deck. They do so. It's the five of hearts. They sign the face of it. You lose their card in the deck. "Wouldn't it be amazing if my dream card was also the five of hearts?" you say, taking out your signed blue-backed card from the envelope again. "Actually, wouldn't it be amazing if my dream card was your *actual signed card.*" You turn your dream card over. It is their signed five of hearts.

Method: You need a red deck and two blue-backed cards. We'll imagine one is the five of hearts. The other can be anything. Now you need to sign the back of both blue-backed cards, and you need to make the signatures look identical. You may have realised by now that the first blue-backed signed card you take out the envelope isn't the same as the one you take out second time.

The random blue-backed card needs to go into the envelope like **pic 1,** *not* the other way around. This means when you open the flap and take out the card the signed back is displayed to the spectators. They can't see the face, for obvious reasons.

Close the flap and put the envelope on the table, flap-side down, as if you were going to write an address. Put the blue five of hearts to the bottom of the red deck.

You are ready to begin. Sit at the table and invite your spectators to sit opposite you. "I had a dream last night," you say. "No, not like that. It was about a card. Bit strange, I agree. But I had to sign the back of it, and I have it in an envelope here." Open the envelope and remove the random blue card, making sure the spectators only see the signed back. "We'll come back to my dream card later." Put it back in the envelope and return it to the tabletop.

"I'd like you to select a card." Pick up the deck, careful not to flash the blue back of the bottom card. "As you can see, this is a red deck." Spread the pack face down, again making sure you don't flash the bottom card. Swing cut and catch a break below the blue five of hearts. You will now perform the riffle force. When they say stop, remove all the cards above the break and turn the whole pile over, displaying the face of the five of hearts. Put the lower packet from your left hand into the middle of the table and hand the permanent marker to a spectator. "Please sign your name across the five of hearts." Hold the packet as they do so. Let the ink dry as you say, "You have chosen and signed the five of hearts. There isn't another like it, would you agree?" Turn your wrist and perform the glide, removing a random card from above the signed five of hearts and placing it atop the packet in the middle of the table. "This is the astonishing thing…"

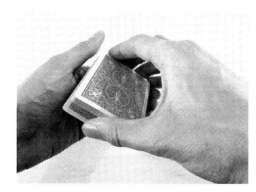

Bring your right hand and left hand together. Readjust so your right fingers and thumb hold the short edges. Now push the bottom card (the signed five of hearts) slightly to the right with your left fingers. Using your little finger, pull down on the flap. Their chosen card will yawn away from the rest of the packet. Hold the position with your right thumb, as in the picture.

Now move your left hand below the table. Bring your right hand down until it's touching the edge of the table, over your lap.

Let the bottom card secretly fall and catch it in your left palm. As you do so bring the right hand packet forward and place it on the pile on the table, supposedly burying the signed five of hearts. As you perform these moves, you say, "The card in my dream was *also* the five of hearts. You don't believe me?"

Scoot the envelope across the table until it's in front of you, and hanging over the edge. You will now press the signed card up against the flap-side of the envelope with your left fingers, and pinch it with your right thumb. Pick up the envelope in your right hand, with the signed five of hearts pinned to the back. You should be looking at the face. Open the flap of the envelope. Insert two fingers inside, but instead of drawing out the random blue card which is still in there, draw the signed five of hearts upwards and into view, as if you pulled it from inside the envelope.

The back will be to the audience, and they will assume it's the card you showed them last time. Put the envelope, flap closed, flap-side down, on the table. "What's even more amazing," you say, "is that my dream card isn't just *any* five of hearts. It's actually *your signed five of hearts*." And turn it round.

SECTION SIX

MENTALISM

Mentalism is the genre of magic related to the mind. Mind reading is an obvious example, but it also includes moving/bending objects with the mind, levitating, and more 'mystic' feats like séances, cold reading and muscle reading. It has been both revolutionised and popularised by the insanely talented Derren Brown, who is so good most magicians (and mentalists) don't have a clue how he does his stuff.

Many feats of mind reading are 'forces', in the same vein as card forces. Forcing bags, dummy pens, that kind of thing. None of the following effects require gimmicks, although there's a section at the end of the book where I discuss further purchases you should think about.

Effect 23

ONE AHEAD

The 'one ahead' principle is a powerful concept. It allows you to discover 'thought of' words with little effort, though does require some presentation.

Effect: The spectator names a wild animal, a city and then selects a card. The magician has correctly predicted every one.

Method: You can probably guess from the description of the effect that a card force is used. But what about the others? This is how it works. You need three pieces of paper, a pen, and a deck of cards with a force card on top. Say the 3 of clubs.

"I'm writing down the name of a wild animal," you say. Hold one piece of paper shielded in your hand so no one else can see what you're writing. Because you are *not* writing down the name of a wild animal. You are writing *3 of clubs*, which is the name of the force card. You screw up the paper into a ball and drop it on the table in front of you. "Please name a wild animal."

It doesn't have to be a wild animal. You can use colours, or names, or pieces of fruit… anything.

The spectator says, "Bear."

Smile. "Outstanding choice!" Pick up another piece of paper. "I'm now writing down the name of a city." Have you guessed what you actually write? You got it. You write the word *Bear*. Screw up the paper and put it in front of the other ball, i.e. a little nearer to you, in a line. The balls should be close to each other. "Okay? Name a city, anywhere in the world."

Hopefully you'll be able to spell it. They say, "New York."

"Never been. You? No? Oh well. Anyway. Lastly, I'm going to write the name of a playing card." And you take the last scrap of paper and write *New York* on it. Screw it up into a ball. Now you will arrange them so. Bring both hands (the *New York* ball is in your right hand) towards the two balls on the table. Clasp both hands over all the balls, hiding them from view as you do this: Drop the ball in your right hand in the middle. Move the front ball (*Bear*) to the left with your left hand and the ball at the back (*3 of clubs*) to the right.

This should take about a second. You will be left with this arrangement, from left to right: Bear, New York, 3 of clubs. This is the order you asked the spectator to name them.

You now need to force the 3 of clubs. Do so now.

"Remember, I made these predictions *before* you said anything out loud and put them on the table. I asked you to name a wild animal. You said 'Bear'. And I wrote…" Unwrap the ball on your left. "I then asked you to name a city. You said 'New York'. I wrote…" Unwrap the middle ball. "Lastly, you picked the 3 of clubs." Unwrap the ball on the right.

Effect 24

<u>SPOON BEND</u>

Spoon bending is a very popular illusion. One of the most famous performers of this effect is Uri Geller. Except he pretends that he really *can* bend spoons with the power of his mind. Which he can't. If you're wondering whether I'm saying Uri is a liar and a fraud… then yes, that's exactly what I'm saying. So sue me, Uri. He even claims to have influenced the outcome of the 2019 General Election by giving Boris Johnson a magic spoon. I'm not even kidding.

Whilst I'm on the subject, anyone who claims real psychic powers to defraud the innocent with hopes of contacting their dead relatives and the like… Well. They're all liars and frauds, using the same techniques mentalists have been using for centuries. Don't fall for it.

Anyway, here's the secret. **The spoon is already bent.**

Get some cheap spoons. The cheaper the better, because they will be flimsy and easier to bend. If you're small, or weak, or both, you can use a tea spoon.

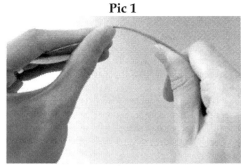

Hold the spoon bowl in you left hand, fingers on top, thumb under. With your right hand bend the stem downwards, like in **pic 1**.

Now, hold the spoon by the stem in your left hand, bowl up and facing out (**pic 2**). Notice that your fingers are not curled. They're stretched out like a wall. And the stem does not extend below your fingers. Also notice that your hand is inclined towards you. This is so that the bowl is vertical and the stem is inclined, rather than the other way round. It should be raised to the eye line of the spectators, and all spectators should be in front of you.

Go stand in front of a mirror and hold the bent spoon as described. Now let the spoon tilt away from you, the bowl moving towards the mirror. To do this you do not rotate your wrist at all. You simply relax your thumb, moving it slowly away from your fingers. The stem will pivot against your index finger. The pictures below are an exposed side view of this motion.

 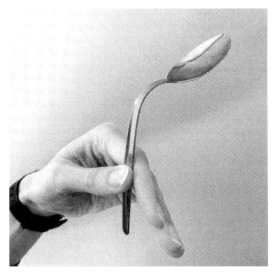

In the mirror, the spoon looks like it is bending, when in reality it is simply being tilted. This is known as the ratcheting illusion.

In performance, have a number of these cheap spoons lying about and ask a spectator to choose one and hand it to you. Gesture with the spoon a bit, as you ask anyone if they're familiar with spoon bending as a psychic power. Most people have heard of the all-powerful psychic spoon bending fraud Uri Geller. Hold it in both hands, bowl in left hand, stem in right, as previously, ready for the bend. Run your right fingers along the top of the stem as you say, "Look, it is perfectly straight at the moment, but watch…"

This is when you secretly do the bend. You clasp the end of the stem in your right hand and bring it towards you, rotating the spoon horizontally, and also move your left hand up, raising the spoon at the same time. In that motion, you quickly apply downward pressure with both hands and bend the spoon.

You then readjust. Your left hand lets go of the bowl and takes the bottom of the stem from your right hand. Now that the spoon is vertical, the slight bend is hidden. Make sure you hold the spoon as directed previously, with the bowl vertical and at the eye line of your spectators.

With your right hand you can add to the illusion. Make a waving, wafting or patting motion above the spoon as you 'bend' it. Or make a beckoning motion beneath the spoon. Bend it *slowly. Very slowly*, hear me?

After you've moved your thumb far enough so that the stem is standing vertical, show the spectators that the spoon has bent a little. Hold it by the bowl in your left hand as before (ready for another bend), showing the bulge in the stem.

This will get a reaction. Now repeat the steps. Bend the spoon again, deeper this time, using the exact hand motions as before. The bowl doesn't need to be exactly vertical this time – the spectators know it is a little bent. Now raise your right hand high above the spoon and bring it quickly down, stopping suddenly about 10cm away as if you've slammed against a mystical force field. 'Bend' the spoon as your right hand shakes with the effort. The illusion is startling.

Effect 25

GHOST TOUCH

This is a beautiful and spooky effect, probably originating around the time of séances and the occult.

Effect: Two spectators sit on chairs a few feet away from each other. They have their eyes shut. The magician touches one of them on the shoulder, and then says, "Can you please raise your arm if you felt something touch you." Both spectators raise their arms.

Method: If you have hundreds to spend on a magic trick, by all means buy a *mentalism chair*. This gimmicked chair shoots a burst of air out of its back rest. If you want to try this effect with two normal chairs on two fairly normal people, read on.

First of all, you *do* actually touch both the spectators, but the audience only sees you touch one of them.

Set up two chairs facing the rest of the audience. The chairs should be a few feet apart and in line with each other. Invite two spectators to take seats. You could choose those who 'have a connection' like partners, or family members, or close friends. Talk about this psychic bond being formed, and how you are going to put it to the test. If there are a pair of twins lying around, by gosh use them.

One spectator sits at **A**, the other sits at **B**. Ask them to sit up straight and close their eyes, and they are only to open their eyes when you say.

They both close their eyes. Now for the secret. You stand between the two chairs and face the audience. **A** is to your right, **B** is to your left. You stand at **A**'s left shoulder. You turn your body and wave your left hand in front of his face, as if checking his eyes are really shut. As you do this, you secretly prod his left shoulder with your right index finger. Your own body, and your turning and waving motion, obscures this from the audience. Also, you will prod him not on top of his shoulder, but on his upper back.

The audience has only seen you wave your hand in front of his face. Now move away from **A**, go over to **B** and openly prod his left shoulder, from above, in an exaggerated motion so the audience can't miss it.

You move back into the middle. "Okay, keep your eyes shut, but please raise your hand if you felt something."

Of course, they will both raise their hands. It won't matter to **A** that you asked the question a while after secretly prodding him.

"Please touch the place where you felt something."

They will both touch their left shoulder. The audience will be suitably amazed.

Effect 26

<u>POCKET WRITING</u>

This is a startling and brilliant concept. Pocket writing is one of the hallmarks of mentalism, along with the nail writer (more on that in the appendix) and the centre tear. The clue is in the name. You secretly write a 'prediction', after the fact, *in your trouser pocket.*

You need a pair of trousers, and you need to be wearing them. Not jeans – jeans' pockets aren't suitable, except for maybe vanishing a coin. The pockets need to be deep and angled, like in any smart work/suit trousers. Banachek advocates wearing a suit jacket too, to help hide the process, but it's not essential.

Now take a pencil, and cut it in half. Be *careful*. The pencil you want should be about 3.5 inches long – about 9cm. Or get a few from IKEA; they're perfect.

You need something flat and sturdy in your pocket to write against, like a piece of plastic or cardboard. Cut a piece from some food packaging, just a little bigger than a playing card. Hey, if your brain's having a slow day and you don't feel creative, you can use an actual playing card. A bit on the flimsy side, but you could make do. Now you need a post-it, so you can stick it to the playing card. Again, a scrap of paper will do but is not so secure.

Fold the post-it in half one way and then the other, in the opposite direction to the sticky so it doesn't stick together. Now unfold it and stick it to the card and put the whole thing in your pocket, the post-it side facing out, so you can write on it when you put your hand in your pocket. Make sure you put it in the pocket corresponding to the hand you write with, won't you? Put the little pencil in there too.

Now put both hands in your pockets. And write a word on the post-it, in your pocket. Do so in front of a mirror. Try to make as little movement as possible, although when you perform this you can have a little walk whilst you do it and no one will notice you fiddling in your pocket (thank heavens).

This will take some practise. You want to be able to write as neatly as possible. Certainly make it legible. Obviously, shorter words are easier than longer ones. Now practise folding the paper up again whilst it's still in your pocket, detaching it and bringing it out into the open. This all needs to be smooth and natural.

Performance:

I like the following presentation. Have the post-it and the pencil ready in your pocket. Hold up your empty hand to the spectators and say, "Here I have an invisible dictionary." Point to a spectator and say, "Please catch it." You 'throw' it to them. Hopefully they'll play along and 'catch' it. "Please open the invisible dictionary anywhere you like."

Now is the time to put your hands in your pockets and grasp the pencil. All eyes will be on your spectator and their invisible dictionary, which they've mimed opening. Unless, of course, you are unlucky enough to have selected someone with no imagination, in which case they may just look at you blankly, and you'll have to ask someone else to take the invisible dictionary from them.

"Look down the page," you say, "and select a word. Think about this for a moment; there are a lot to choose from. But select a shortish word – no more than six or seven letters. Got one? Okay, tell me what the word is."

The word could almost be anything. Let's imagine they say *chalk*. You say, "Chalk? Interesting. Any reason why you chose that word? Did it just jump out at you?"

And as you speak you also take a few steps to either the right (if you're right handed) or left (if you're left handed), which turns your pencil pocket away from the spectators, and you write the word *chalk* on the paper.

"Okay, excellent. Throw the invisible dictionary back to me." And you take your hands out of your pockets (both empty) and catch it as they throw it back to you. Or you could duck, or let it sail over your head or into a corner and tell them they missed or it was a bad throw or whatever.

Now for the reveal. You put your hands back in your pockets again and take a few steps around, and you say, "Earlier today the strangest thing happened. A word just kept popping into my mind, over and over again. In fact, I had to write it down in the end. I didn't know why. But now I do."

And here are some options.

Reveal 1

Whilst speaking, you need to fold the post-it up and detach it and hold it tight in your fingers (like a coin in finger palm). You say, "The piece of paper is in my jacket pocket." Open your jacket with your free hand, directing the spectators' eyes there. Bring the hand with the paper straight out of your trousers at the same time, and into your jacket pocket. Produce the folded post-it.

Reveal 2

This is my preferred presentation. Go out and buy a pack of really little envelopes, as little as you can get, that will fit in a trouser pocket. If possible, the flap should be at the short end rather than the long edge, but you gotta make do with what you can get. The front of the envelope is where you'd write the address. The back is where you seal the flap down. You're going to cut out a large portion of the front, creating a *window envelope*.

If using scissors: open the envelope as wide as possible, and give the middle of the front of the envelope a pinch with your fingers. Now cut a slit in that fold. You will now be able to cut into the front of the envelope, albeit in a kind of spiral like a snail shell. Cut out most of the front of the envelope, leaving a border at least 1cm thick all the way round.

If using a craft knife: slide some cardboard into the envelope to protect the back. Slice a window out of the front of the envelope, leaving at least a 1cm border.

Now cut a piece of paper to the perfect size for the envelope and slide it in. It should slide in and out with little effort, but fill the window. Now seal the envelope. Put the sealed window envelope into your pocket, against the sturdy support (piece of cardboard/plastic etc.), with the window facing out. Instead of writing on a post-it, you will write on the piece of paper *through* the window in the envelope. Can you see how startling this reveal will be?

"The piece of paper is in a sealed envelope in my pocket," you say, taking out the envelope. You must turn your palm up as you are taking it out to present the sealed back. Your hand will cover most of the window, but you want to avoid any flashes. Open the flap without tearing it off. If you need to lay the envelope on a table to do this, fine. Ensure the front window is facing the floor. Pull out the paper inside and crumple the envelope up as soon as it's free and put it back in your pocket. Turn the paper over for all to see.

Reveal 3

This reveal is from inside your wallet. The advantage is that the wallet itself acts as a sturdy support to write against. We'll say the front of the wallet is the side with the buckle or latch. To open it you need to pop the buckle at the front. You will write against the *back*. Do not use a post-it – you don't want it sticking. Just use a small piece of paper. Make sure the wallet doesn't have any coins in it. It needs to be as flat as possible so as not to take up too much pocket space.

Put the wallet in your pocket, buckle facing in, paper facing out. Write on the paper and fold it up as described previously.

"The piece of paper is folded up in my wallet," you say, and take it out of your pocket. Your fingers conceal the folded paper, holding it against the back of the wallet. This is why we haven't used a post-it; it would stick. Pop the buckle, open the wallet, and then open the large sleeve pocket at the back (where you put notes) with both thumbs, keeping the folded paper pressed against the back. Lift the hand with the paper (the paper held in finger palm) and push your fingers deep into the cash sleeve. Do NOT fiddle with the paper *until* your fingers are deep inside. Push the paper to the end of your fingers with your thumb and withdraw it.

NOTES: There are lots of presentations that utilize pocket writing – you don't need to use an invisible dictionary:

BOOK TEST: Let the spectator choose an actual book from their library, or from a pile you've brought with you. Let them turn to any page and select any word from the page (as long as it's short – "no more than six or seven letters.").

NAME THAT NAME: Ask a spectator to think of a person's name – just their first name - it can be someone close to them, a celebrity, or any random name they come up with.

YOUR NUMBER'S UP: It doesn't have to be a word, of course! Why not ask a spectator to name a four or five digit number. You could have a few spectators choose a digit each. If you're really good at maths, try the following: say, "I have a number written down…" and ask a spectator to write down a two (or three if you're a whiz) digit number on a white board, nice and big. Look at what they've written. "Agh, sorry, that's not the number I've got, I'll try another person, I'm sorry about that." Ask another spectator to write down a two digit number underneath the first. "Oh no! It's not that either!" you say, and now you're frantically adding the two numbers together and pocket writing the total. You then say, "Ah! But look… if we add these two numbers together we get this… which is the number I have written down…"

SECTION SEVEN

MORE CARD SLEIGHTS

The False Overhand Shuffle With Injog

Sounds confusing, doesn't it. I'm afraid it is, a little. And it's not easy, either. But it's worth the effort, because there are effects where you will need to false shuffle a card second from the top, or a few cards, instead of just the top card. If you do need to false shuffle the deck keeping just the top card in position, we've already learnt how to do that. Shuffle the single card to the bottom and then to the top again. This is for the occasions when that is not enough.

You can retain the top few cards in position with a **false cut** instead, of course. Swing cut the pack and catch a break as you replace the cards in your right hand on top. Speak for a moment, gesturing with your right hand, distracting the spectators. Now cut off half the upper packet and put it on the table. Not cut off the rest of the upper packet (every card above the break) and put that onto the tabled cards. Now place the lower packet (the remaining cards in your left hand) on top of that. The top half of the pack will remain unchanged.

Now let's get on with learning the false overhand shuffle with injog. Easy for me to say, right? Deposit the first packet into your left hand, and raise the rest of the pack in your right hand in a chopping motion as you would a normal shuffle. But the second deposit is not going to go directly on top of the cards in your left hand, as it would in a normal shuffle. You will *injog* the second packet, about half an inch towards you, as in **pic 1** below. Just deposit a few cards (or even just one). Shuffle the remaining cards on top in a haphazard fashion, hiding the jog. If you turn the deck upright you'll see the face of the jogged card (8 of clubs here) in **pic 2**.

Pic 1

Pic 2

From this position you have two options; do you cut or do you shuffle?

Cut: Put your right thumb tip against the jogged 8 of clubs and lift off the entire packet behind it (marked **X** in **pic 1**). This was the original top packet.

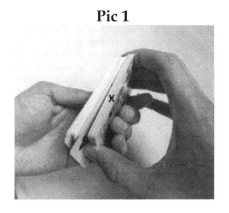
Pic 1

This packet gets dumped on top of all the other cards, i.e. to the left.

Shuffle: More difficult, but stronger. Instead of picking up the back packet, you're going to shuffle off the front packet first. Instead of putting your thumb tip against the jogged 8 of clubs, you're going to press it against the very edge, beveling it back as in **pic 2**.

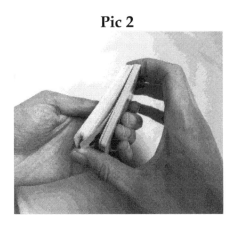
Pic 2

Now squeeze your thumb and fingers together, creating a neat little tent (**pic 3**). Lift your right hand, letting a small number of cards fall from the left packet into your left palm (**pic 4**). Lift your right hand free and chop it down in front of these cards, depositing more from the left packet, as you would a normal shuffle (**pic 5**). You will shuffle all the cards off the left packet, and then put the right packet (the original top packet) down on top of them all in its entirety.

Pic 3

Pic 4

Pic 5

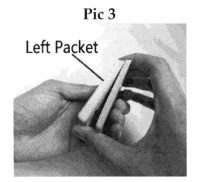
Left Packet

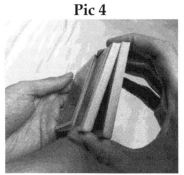

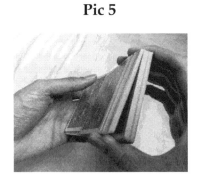

The Marlo Tilt

The Marlo Tilt (named after its inventor, Ed Marlo) is one of the most effective card controls. It appears that you insert a chosen card into the middle of the deck when in fact it goes in second from the top. Here's how.

Pic 1

Pic 2

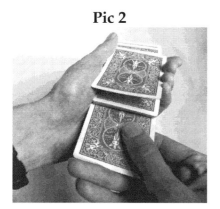

Have a card selected and withdrawn. Whist the card is being looked at, hold the deck in your left hand in mechanic's grip. Square the pack with your right hand and in doing so lift up the top card with your right thumb. Rest it upon your left little finger and the heel of your left thumb, so it is raised a little, like a break, but with the whole card raised instead of just a corner. The front of the card should remain flush with the deck (**pic 1**).

You will now take the chosen card with your right hand and *pretend* to push it into the middle of the deck. Take the card *behind* the back of the deck and push it a little way into the middle. This pushes a few cards from the middle out the front of the deck for the spectator to see (**pic 2**). Then take the chosen card and put it under just the *top* card, which is slightly lifted, squaring the deck as you do so. The spectator thinks it went into the middle when in reality it is second from the top.

Effect 27

<u>CARD IN BOX</u>

Effect: A card is selected and inserted into the middle of the deck. It magically jumps to the top when the magician taps the deck. To make it harder, the magician inserts the card and then puts the card box on top of the deck. He taps the card box. Has the chosen card jumped to the top of the deck? No. It's now actually inside the card box.

Method: A duplicate card is needed. Let's say it's the 6 of diamonds. Put one 6 of diamonds in the card box. Put the other on top of the deck, and then force it on a spectator at the start of the trick.

Marlo tilt the 'chosen' 6 of diamonds into the deck, second from top. The spectator will believe it's lost somewhere in the middle. "Now watch," you say. "If we take the top card…" – take the top card and turn it over. Let's say it's the jack of clubs, but it could be anything. "… which obviously is *not* your card -" It's not, it's the jack of clubs. Their 6 of diamonds is *now* on top. Tap the deck with one corner of the jack of clubs. "If we tap the deck look what happens… your card jumps to the top."

Lay the jack of clubs face up on the table and turn over the top card, showing it is indeed the 6 of diamonds.

"Wait, there's more." Allow the spectator to insert the 6 of diamonds into the deck anywhere, losing it somewhere in the middle. "We will make it more difficult." Put the card box on top of the deck, careful not to rattle the duplicate inside. "Now the magic has to pass through the card box as well as the deck."

Yeah right. Pick up the jack of clubs and tap a corner on top of the card box. Then take the box off the deck and hand it to a spectator. "Hold this."

With trembling hands you turn over the top card of the deck. It is not their chosen 6 of diamonds. Oh dear. But wait! You look at the card box, which is held by a spectator. "Hold on. Just give the box a shake for me."

They shake the box. Something rattles inside. They open it. Voila. "It must have jumped *through* the cardboard into the box!" Of course it must.

Effect 28

<u>CARD AT ANY NUMBER</u>

This is my version of CAAN (card at any number), a standard in card magic.

Effect: A spectator selects a card – a prediction - which is placed face down on the table without anyone looking at it. They then select another card, which they look at and remember. It is returned to the deck and shuffled in. The prediction card is then turned over. It is a five. Five cards are counted from the top of the deck. The fifth card is the spectator's chosen card.

Method: You need to force any five. You can use any number card you wish, but the lower the number the easier the handling. Say you riffle force the five. Place it face down on the table without anyone seeing. "This will be a prediction," you say. "We'll come back to it later."

Turn to another spectator and say, "I'd like you to pick a card now please." Spread the cards in your hands and allow them to freely select one. However, that's not all you do. When you spread the cards you need to count four cards from the top (the right). When the spectator selects one, you need to square the pack, but you *must catch a break beneath the fourth card*. Do this by pressing your right index finger against the face of (beneath) the fourth card, like a marker, whilst you spread out the cards. Then when you square the deck you must push up against this card, allowing your left little finger to sneak under it.

Whilst the selected card is being shown about, you need to set up for the Marlo tilt. But instead of tilting just the top card, you are going to tilt up all four cards above the break. You take back the selected card and perform the tilt as normal, prodding out a few cards from the middle and then sliding it under the four card packet. So the selected card goes fifth from the top.

Now give the pack a false shuffle, retaining the top packet as described, with the injog (or give it a swing cut/cut to table combo if you prefer). Place the pack on the table.

"Okay, now we can look at the card you first selected. I said it would be a prediction. We are not interested in the suit, only the number. Please turn it over. Okay, it's a five." You point to the deck. "Please deal four cards and then turn over the fifth."

Matt Walker's Roundhouse Glide

Is it narcissistic to name a card sleight after yourself? Possibly. I considered a few different names when I invented this useful technique. The Side Glide. The Side Swipe. But I settled on the Roundhouse Glide because the motion resembles a roundhouse kick, which sounds cool.

Pic 1

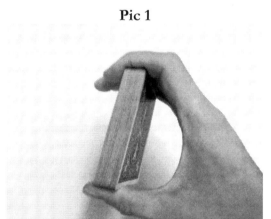

Hold the deck by its short edges in your right hand, face card facing out as in **pic 1**. Thumb underneath. Fingers on top, with the tips of your middle and ring fingers extended past the first joint (just like the standard glide).

This means you can bend these fingers over and clasp against the face card, as in **pic 2**. Now pull down on your bottom three fingers and the face card will swing out towards your palm (**pic 3**). This exposes a bit of the face of the second card from the bottom (in this case, the 8 of spades). If you tilt your wrist down now, the jutted out glided card is hidden by the back of your hand.

Pic 2

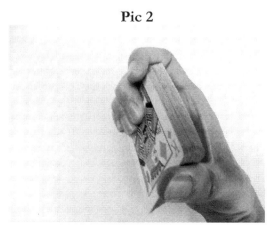

Pic 3

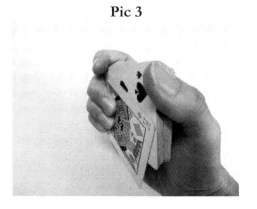

There are a few applications, the most useful being a convincing card control:

Convincing Control

This is a beautiful control of a freely selected card, even if I do say so myself. It looks like the card goes in the middle, sticking out the deck, when really it goes to the bottom of the pack.

Hold the deck in your left hand. There are a number of ways the spectator can freely select the card, allowing you into the *'get ready'*. You can riffle down the deck and ask the spectator to say stop – and you really *do* stop where they tell you. Lift off the top packet with your right, holding it in position for the roundhouse glide as shown previously in **pic 1 & 2**. Show them the face of the packet, which is the card they stopped you at.

Or you can hold the deck flat in your left hand and tell them to lift off a packet of cards from the top. They lift off a packet. You take it off them with your right hand, show them the face and get it in position for the roundhouse glide.

Now, this is important. Let's imagine their chosen card is the ace of spades.

It is on the face of the packet in your right hand, facing the spectator. You hold the bottom half of the deck in your left hand. Extend your left index and middle fingers and bring them to the face of the ace of spades, as in the adjacent picture (this is from the magician's point of view).

You are going to pretend to slide off the ace of spades. In reality, you are going to take the card just behind it. Tilt both hands down. Your left fingers are still touching the face of the ace of spades. Perform the roundhouse glide, now hidden from the spectators, and withdraw the indifferent card with your left fingers. **Pic 4** below is what you will see. **Pic 5** is the exposed view from underneath.

Pic 4

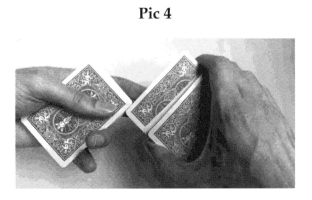

Pic 5

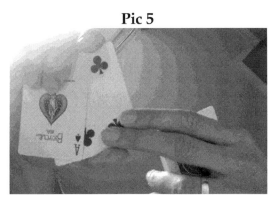

The indifferent card is slid out on top of the lower packet in your left hand. Use your left thumb to peel it off. Let it protrude off the front edge (**pic 6**). Now slightly relax your right fingers (the three holding the glided ace of spades). Let the ace of spades tilt downwards off the bottom of the pack as in **pic 7**. Slide the right packet on top of the left, with the sagging ace of spades going to the very bottom of the deck (**pic 8**). Square the pack, keeping the indifferent card protruding out, as in **pic 9**. The spectators think the protruding card is the ace of spades, when really it's on the bottom of the deck.

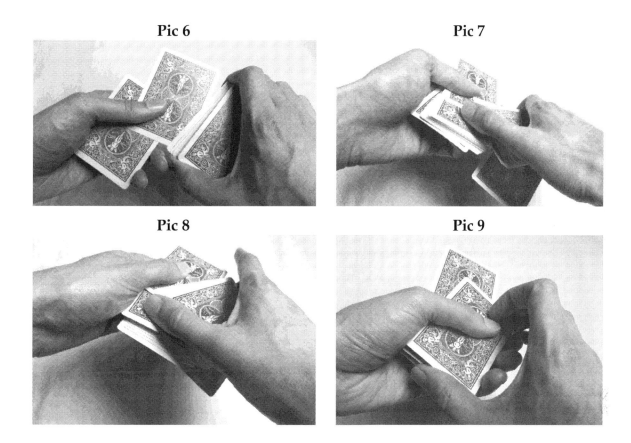

Pic 6

Pic 7

Pic 8

Pic 9

Effect 29

ACE SHAKE

This is my version of the famous *Ace Shake*, popularised by David Blaine amongst others.

Effect: You hand the spectator the two red aces, and then get them to select a card, look at it and remember it. They can even sign the face of it in permanent marker. Their card is lost in the deck. You take back the two red aces and hand the deck to the spectator. You wave the red aces over the pack and *presto!* A card appears magically between them. It is their signed chosen card.

Method: Okay, I prefer to use the two jokers, but *Joker Shake* doesn't have as nice a ring to it. I will, to avoid confusion, use the red aces in this explanation. Take the red aces out of the deck and hand them to a spectator. Now ask another spectator to select a card from the deck. It is a perfectly free selection. They can even sign the face of the card. Now take their chosen card back, apparently lose it in the deck but really control it to the bottom. You can do that using my roundhouse glide convincing control, or if that is a little tricky for the moment, first control the card to the top using a break and false cut or false shuffle, and then shuffle it to the bottom. Make sure you don't flash anything to the spectators.

Now you need to get a break above the bottom (chosen) card, like in the opposite picture. Here's how. Hold the deck in your left hand and bring your right hand over it, as if you've just squared the pack, which you might have just done. Push the bottom card slightly to the right with your left fingers. Now using your little finger, pull down on the flap.

The bottom card will yawn away from the rest of the deck. If you wanted, you could let it fall into your left palm. Instead, hold the break in position with your **right** thumb and lift the pack away with your right hand, as in the picture. The spectators will be unaware of this break, because the front of the deck is still flush.

Now ask the spectator with the red aces to inspect them. "You just have the two normal red aces?" you say. And they answer yes. Hold out your left hand and ask for them back. If they give them to you face-up, flip them over with your fingers. You need to hold both aces face-down and squared together in mechanic's grip in your left hand.

Now here is where the magic happens. "Take the deck," you say. And you bring your right hand (which has the deck) forward, and you bring your left hand with the aces back towards you. You bring the deck directly over your left hand, maybe an inch above it. And you secretly drop the bottom card on top of the aces. Do not hesitate or halt mid-movement. It has to happen in one flowing, natural motion. The chosen card will go onto the aces, and you need to square the packet immediately with your left thumb and fingers so no one will notice the added card. You do this as you hand the deck to the spectator.

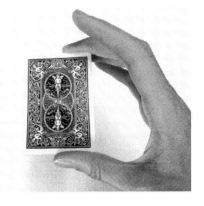

"You have the deck, I have the two red aces," you say. Take the three-card packet in your right hand like in the opposite picture, face-down. Peel off the bottom ace with your left fingers, holding the remaining two cards as one. Turn the left hand ace *face-up* and put it on top of the two cards in your right hand. Now peel off the other red ace from the bottom, just as before, and turn it face-up.

This time, the right hand cards go on top of the left hand ace (which is face-up). This sandwiches the spectator's chosen card face-down in the middle of the two face-up aces.

Now take the three-card packet in your right hand as before and use your left fingers to peel out the bottom ace. But don't take it all the way off; just slide it a centimetre to the left, keeping the other two cards flush.

Now readjust your grip, so you're holding the cards pinched between your right thumb and index finger like the opposite picture.

Now quickly wave the cards over the deck held by the spectator. As you do so, simply press down firmly with your thumb and the top two cards will spread apart. Slow to a stop and show that a face-down card has 'jumped' from the deck between the aces. Let the spectator remove and turn it over.

The Top Change

This is a useful card sleight, but it requires misdirection and timing. i.e. The spectator should not be looking at your hands when you do this sleight, or they might notice something 'dodgy' going on. Basically, you hold the deck in your left hand, a chosen card in your right hand, and you quickly change the chosen card for the top card of the deck without anyone noticing. Sound impossible? Well, that's why you don't want anyone burning your hands with their eyes.

Hold the deck in left hand mechanic's grip. Take any card and hold it in your right hand, pinched between your thumb and index finger as in **pic 1** on the next page. Notice that the left thumb has pushed the top card of the deck over to the right.

This is where the misdirection comes in. **I only use the top change when I can gesture at something with the card in my right hand.** Say there's another card on the table. Gesture to it with the card pinched in your right hand. "Turn it over," you say, and all eyes will go to the card on the table as it is turned over. You will be free to perform the following top change thus: Gesture with the card you're holding in your right hand (we'll call this card **A**), and as you do so, push over the top card of the deck (we'll call this card **B**) with your left thumb (**pic 1**). When all eyes are off you and on the tabled card, bring your right hand back towards you and to the deck. Slide your right hand card (**A**) on top of the beveled top card of the deck (**B**). Your right fingers slide below the top card **B** (**pic 2**). Now swap them. Your left thumb takes card **A** from your right hand, and your right fingers and thumb take away the top card **B** (**pic 3**). This should be done in a smooth, slick motion. As far as the spectators are concerned, all you did was lean forward and gesture with a card in your right hand, and then lean back again. They don't realise the top change has occurred.

| **Pic 1** | **Pic 2** | **Pic 3** |

Effect 30

LIGHTNING CARD

One of the best tricks in *The Royal Road To Card Magic* is this one. Hugard and Braue's version requires a palm however. My version uses the top change instead.

Effect: The spectator thinks of a number between 5 and 15, remembers the card at that number, and then even sees their chosen card in the top half of the deck, which is handed to them. The spectator and magician both deal out cards up to that chosen number. But, at the end, it's the *magician* who holds the selected card, not the spectator.

Method: Ask the spectator to shuffle the pack, and then to secretly think of a number between 5 and 15. Take the shuffled deck back. "I am going to show you the cards one by one, and I want you to remember the card at your chosen number. Can you do that?"

They should say yes. If they say no, find someone who can count to 15. Now thumb over the top card, pick it up with your right hand and display the face to the spectator, without looking at it yourself. "1," you say. Bring it back to the deck as you thumb over the second card. You pick up both cards together and display the face of the second card. "2." Bring the two-card packet back to the deck and pick up the third card as well and display that. "3." Notice that you don't change the order of the cards. Repeat until you have shown 15 cards, then put the 15-card packet back on top.

"You remembered the card at your number?"

They say they did, which is good. You are now going to perform the *backslip*. Hold the deck in left hand mechanic's grip. With your right hand grasp about half the pack. You will appear to lift this top half away. However, when you do so your left thumb squeezes against the top card. It secretly slides off onto the left hand packet (see pictures below).

Whilst you execute the backslip, turn slightly, showing the back of your left hand to your spectators. This keeps the sleight hidden. Put the left hand lower packet on the table. Remember you backslipped the top card on top of it. You now spread the cards in your right hand, which is the top half. Have the faces displayed to the spectator, and ask if he sees his card. He does, but unbeknown to him it is now one card higher in the packet than he thinks it is.

Hand him the top half. "You are positive your card is in there? You can double check."

Perhaps he double checks, perhaps he does not. Then ask him what number he chose. "Not the card, just the number."

Imagine he says 12. "Okay, good," you say. "We are going to deal the cards out now, like this." Pick up the top card from the pile on the table with your right hand and put it in your left. "1," you say. Now offer your left hand and say, "Deal your top card on top of mine."

The spectator does so. Then pick up another card from the tabled pile and put that on top of the two cards in your left hand. "2." Gesture for the spectator to do the same. Continue dealing the cards out in this manner, all the cards face down. When you get to 11 (one less than the chosen number), notice that the card the spectator puts into your left hand *is actually his chosen card*. But he thinks his chosen card will be the 12th card.

"And 12 was the number you chose?" you say, and you pick up the 12th card from the pile on the table and keep it in your right hand.

The spectator confirms yes it was. "What card was it?" you ask. Let's say the spectator says it was the five of diamonds. "Turn it over," you say, and you gesture at him with the card in your right hand. All eyes go to the spectator turning over his 12th card. You bring your right hand back and top change the card you hold for the top card in your left hand packet. Remember, *this* is the chosen card.

The spectator turns over an indifferent card and looks confused.

"Ah," you say, "you see – the five of diamonds wasn't *your* 12th card… it's mine." And turn over the card in your right hand.

SECTION EIGHT

MISC.

Effect 31

ARM TWIST ILLUSION

Popularised by Shinkoh Nagisa (who apparently learnt it off a circus performer), the arm twist illusion is striking and impromptu, meaning you can perform it anytime, anywhere (as long as you have long sleeves. And arms). It has been performed by both David Blaine and David Copperfield. And soon you.

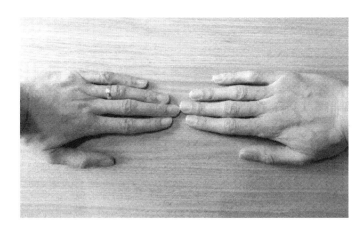

Effect: Go to a table (or a wall) and put your hands against the surface like the opposite picture. Now look at your right hand. Try moving it round in a circle – *anticlockwise* (that's downwards first). Impossible, right?

Well, yes. That's why some trickery is involved.

Method: The secret is in the way you put your right hand on the table. Put your hands out in front of you now, palms up, as if you're trying to stop a speeding truck. Now rotate your hands down to imitate the above picture. Your left hand moves clockwise, your right hand moves anticlockwise. Right? Natural. And that's what the spectator *assumes* you do. But it is not.

Go to a table (you can also do it against a wall, but I'll use a table for the description). Your hands hang at your sides. Now rotate your right hand so your palm touches the table edge (**pic 1** following page. I am not wearing long sleeves, you'll notice. This is so you can clearly see the movement. During performance <u>you must wear long sleeves</u>). Press your fingers against the tabletop and rotate your arm, so your palm moves out to the right (**pic 2**). Carry round the rotation (**pic 3**). Finally, press your palm (**gently!**) against the tabletop. You must be really careful not to hyperextend your wrist. If you feel any pain or discomfort, discontinue learning the effect. Your hands will look like **pic 4**, which has an uncanny resemblance to the picture at the top of this page. The difference, is that in pic 4 your right arm has already been rotated. The effect simply involves *un*-rotating it.

Pic 1   **Pic 2**

Pic 3   **Pic 4**

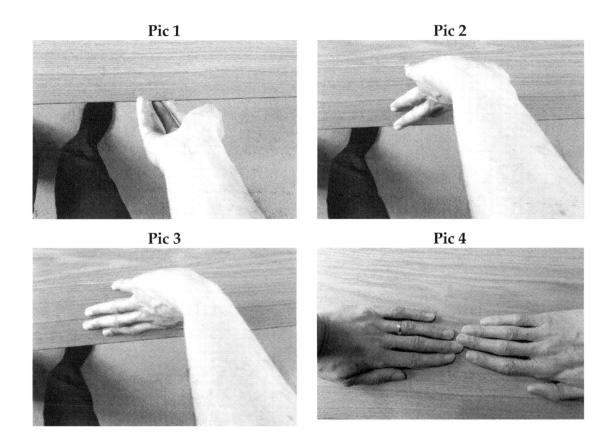

With your hands setup thus, you will find you can easily rotate your right hand anticlockwise, a feat that seems impossible. Make sure you wear long sleeves, else the spectators might notice your elbow pointing in the wrong direction (!).

In performance, you can simply walk the spectators to a table. Make sure you get there first, mind. Then get into position whilst they're still crowding around you. "Put your hands on the table like me," you say. They will undoubtedly assume the position in the way any normal person would. "Try and copy what I do," you say. Perform the illusion slowly, at first. They'll be able to move maybe an inch or two. But then proceed with the rotation, 360°, all the way round.

LEVITATIONS

You can levitate yourself or you can levitate objects. Not literally, of course, but you can make it look like you can. Unfortunately, the vast majority of object levitations require something called *invisible thread*. It is basically thread that is so thin it is almost invisible, even up close. Magician's stick this thread to their thumbnail using wax, and the other end to an object, and they pass the thread over their other hand, like a pulley system (or sometimes over their *head*). Moving your hand makes the object rise and fall, apparently floating. It is a truly beautiful illusion, and you should look into buying some if this interests you (although it is not easy). See the appendix for recommendations into further purchases.

For now, however, I want to introduce you to a small object levitation I invented, which I imaginatively named *Float*.

Effect 32

<u>FLOAT</u>

This works best with a small soft fruit, like a ripe plum or kiwi fruit or orange. You need a fairly long, sharp pencil. And a small soft fruit, obvs. Oh, and a watch. If you don't wear watches, you should try one, they're really useful. I mean, you *could* use a couple of tight hair bands on your wrist, if your fashion sense can pull it off. Or long sleeves with tight cuffs, or a hidden elastic band. But a watch works best.

You've probably seen the pictures below and realised the secret. You stick the pencil inside your watch strap, like **pic 1**, so it looks like a gauntlet blade from *Assassins Creed*, but not quite as cool. You can actually hold your hand quite naturally from the front without the pencil being seen. Pick up a piece of fruit, and jam it onto the end of the pencil. You may need to brace the pencil with your right thumb. You can do this in full view of the spectator in the pretence of 'feeling' it. ("I just need to check it's not too dense, or too heavy, alright?")

Hold your arm out, so it's level with your spectator's eyes. The fruit rests in your palm. Put your other hand over it, and give a funny wave. By bending your left wrist down and performing a waving up/down motion with both hands, it'll look like the fruit is floating. **Pic 2** exposed view. **Pic 3** from the front (nice tie).

Pic 1

Pic 3

Pic 2

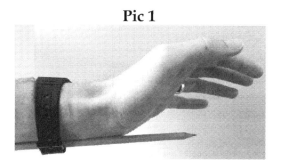

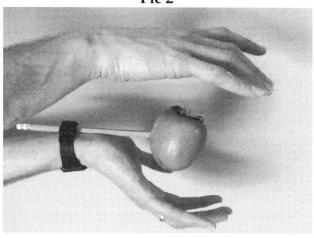

(That thing's a persimmon by the way,
if you're wondering)

Effect 33

<u>THE BALDUCCI LEVITATION</u>

Probably the most popular (and arguably the best) self-levitation there is. Whilst others require shoes to be taken on and off, secretly standing on small objects dropped from the trouser leg, or suspended on (supposedly invisible) wires, this levitation is entirely impromptu. It does have its limitations, including serious angle issues, but hey, it's this or nothing.

Ed Balducci didn't actually invent this levitation (its originator is unknown) but he popularised it.

Basically, you stand on one foot, and the angles make it look like you're floating.

Go stand in front of a mirror. Now raise yourself onto your right foot tiptoes. *Just* your right foot tiptoes. Your left leg stays perfectly straight, and your left foot stays parallel to the floor. That's not fooling anybody, right? Right. But look at the adjacent picture. More convincing, isn't it. This is the optimum angle. The spectator stands at your 7 or 8 o'clock. When you raise yourself onto your tiptoe, your right foot is hidden by your left leg and left foot.

You need to be perhaps ten to fifteen feet from a spectator, and the fewer spectators the better. Just one is ideal. Put your arms out, part for balance, part for effect, and raise them slightly as you 'raise' up.

SECTION NINE

COIN ROUTINES

We learnt basic coin handling in Section Four. Now's the time to look at a couple of routines.

Effect 34

COINS ACROSS

Effect: Simple yet effective. The teleportation of three coins one-by-one from one hand to the other… and it uses *only* three coins.

Method: Have three two pence pieces lying on the table and show your hands empty back and front. Pick up one of the coins with your left fingers and put it in your right palm <u>in position for the classic palm.</u> You don't actually palm it yet; just place it in the correct position. Now put a second coin on top, overlapping, and then the third coin on top of that (**pic 1** below).

Pic 1

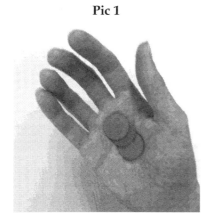

"Three coins," you say, "go into my left hand." And you tip your right hand over your left, depositing two coins *but retaining the third in classic palm.* The spectators believe, of course, that your left hand contains all three. You close your left hand, then close your right. Do some kind of squeezing motion, then produce the palmed coin at the tips of your right fingers. Then open your left hand to show only two coins. Tip the two coins from your left hand onto the table. "One coin jumps," you say.

Traditionally, the next coin across would be accomplished with the *click pass*. This involves 'tipping' a coin into your left, but really classic palming it, then picking up a second coin with the right fingers and apparently dropping that into the left hand 'too'. But you actually release the classic palmed coin, it clinks off the other coin at your fingertips and goes into your left hand. Then you steal the second coin away in right hand finger palm. I am not a huge fan of the click pass, so I use this method, which is simpler and as good, and still produces a nice clink.

You still hold a coin in your right hand. Tip it *for real* into your left palm. Flash your palm to show it's really there – but do it subtly! Now pick up one of the coins from the table with your right fingers. Let it fall into your **right** palm, and shake your hand a little to get it into position for the classic palm. Now tip your right hand over your left, apparently dropping it in as well. However, retain it in classic palm, and bump your palms together (hard) so the coin in your left hand jumps and clinks against the coin classic palmed in your right. Same effect, smoother execution. You'll end up with one coin in your left hand (the spectators believe there're two) and one coin classic palmed in your right, which the spectators believe to be empty.

Close your left hand into a fist and pick up the remaining coin from the table with your right fingers. "Two coins in my left, one in my right." Close your right fist, being sure to keep the coin you just picked up at your fingers so the two coins don't 'talk'. Squeeze your left, then shake your right sharply, relaxing your palm. If you're lucky, the two coins in your right hand will clink together in your fist.

Open your left hand to show one coin, open your right hand to show two. "One jumps. Lastly…" Put the two coins from your right hand on the table, so they're overlapping one on top of the other. You're now going to vanish the coin in your left hand. You can either do it using the classic palm vanish again (right hand retains it in classic palm as you 'tip it' into your left) or by using the French drop, in which case the coin remains in your left hand. I use the French drop, as you should usually try to use different methods when repeating vanishes etc.

Whichever method you use, one hand will have the coin secretly palmed in it. It is this hand that scoops up the two coins from the table. All the coins can jingle merrily together, as two coins jingling sounds just like three. Close your fists. Reveal that one hand is empty and the other has all three coins.

Effect 35

<u>SALT AND PEPPER</u>

Effect: A three-part routine involving a copper coin and a silver coin.

Method: Firstly, you need to be sitting at a table, and you need a duplicate silver coin sitting on your left knee (sorry). I use a 10p (silver) and 2p (copper). Only the copper coin requires a palm, so use any suitable currency.

The first part involves taking both coins in one hand and having the copper coin magically jump to the other. There are two ways of doing this. You can do my alternative to the *click pass* from the previous effect: really tip the silver coin into the left hand, and then classic palm the copper coin when you pretend to tip that one in also, making sure they *clink* together (or you could do the *actual* click pass).

Or you could have the silver coin resting atop the copper coin in your right hand, and when you tip 'both' coins into your left hand you retain the copper in classic palm, only letting the silver one tip (just like the first part of the previous effect *Coins Across*, but with two coins instead of three).

In any case, you say, "I have a silver coin and a copper coin. Both go into my left hand." You end up with the silver coin in your left and the copper coin secretly classic palmed in your right. Close both fists and give them a little magic shake. "Now watch what happens…" I like to give my hand a little jerk, and 'throw' the coin to my fingertips, pinching it between fingers and thumb, as if it appears there. It's a cool little flourish, but if you prefer you can just open your hands. Do so left hand first, then right hand. "The copper coin jumps!" you say.

Now for the second jump. Tip the copper coin from your right hand onto the table, then take the silver coin between both hands' fingertips and manipulate it. Do so naturally, as if you're just playing with the coin. Then perform the French drop, pretending to take it in your right hand but actually retaining it in finger palm in your left. Close your right hand into a fist and pick up the copper coin from the table with your left fingers, careful not to flash the palmed 10p. Close your left fist, careful not to clink the coins together. Give your hands a shake and reveal that, "This time the silver coin jumps!"

You can of course perform the classic palm vanish again, if you prefer, but it is usually better to mix up your vanishing methods.

Now for the last part of the trick. Put both coins down in front of you on the table, and then put both hands into your lap. "So we've seen the copper coin jump, and we've seen the silver coin jump." As you say this, pick up the duplicate silver coin from your left knee and loosely hold it in left finger palm. Now bring both hands back to the tabletop.

Do you remember the *coin to small object transformation*? You are going to perform the same moves now. Pick up the copper coin with your right hand thus: put your right fingers on top of the coin and slide it towards you, to the edge of the table. Then pinch it from underneath with your thumb as you slide it over the edge. Lift it up and then left it fall into your right palm, in position for classic palm.

Open your left hand – but don't let anyone see the duplicate silver coin! – and pretend to tip the copper coin into it, but actually retain it in right hand classic palm. Close your left hand. Everyone believes it has the copper coin in it, when in actuality it has the duplicate silver coin.

Now you will pretend to pick up the remaining silver coin from the table top. Place your right fingers on top of the coin and slide it across the table towards you (remember, you have the copper coin classic palmed as you do this). You will pretend to pinch the silver coin between your thumb and fingers, just like you did with the copper coin a moment ago. This time, however, you simply slide it off the table and into your lap. Pretend to pinch the coin and raise your hand, letting the coin fall. The spectators think it is at your fingertips. Now close your fist.

"First we saw the copper coin jump. Then we saw the silver coin jump. This time…" And open your hands. "*Both* coins have jumped, and changed places!"

Effect 36

<u>BARE NAKED COIN MATRIX</u>

Effect: Another staple of coin magic, the coin matrix involves four coins set out in a square. The coins are covered, usually with cards, and shown to jump magically about until they are all assembled in one corner. My version uses just the magician's hands for cover. No one needs to be naked.

Method: I don't want you to feel sorry for me, but this routine took years. You need five coins. Yes, I said five. Sorry. Four of them are set out on the table in a square. The fifth is classic palmed in your right hand. Again, sorry. Don't let anyone see the fifth coin, will you. The table needs to have a cloth on it. There will be some sliding going on, and you don't want anyone to hear it.

So, the coins on the table are set out in a square. Top left, top right, bottom right, bottom left, going clockwise as you look at it. You are going to cover the bottom left coin with your left hand. Then cover the top right coin with your right hand. And as you move your right hand up across the table, you inch your left hand up slightly until you can touch the coin with the heel of your hand. Move it back so it's in line with the bottom right coin, if need be, scooting the coin with you.

The first vanish is simple yet effective. Drop the palmed coin from your right hand next to the top right coin – don't let them clink! You will now do the reveal with both hands at the same time. Do so by spreading out your thumbs to make an L and slightly moving your hands back towards you, on a diagonal. Your right hand reveals two coins. Your left reveals nothing, because the coin is trapped under the heel of your hand. Bring your left hand to the edge of the table. Now leave the coin there, on the table edge, and move your hand forward again. Your wrist and forearm hides the stolen coin. Turn your hand over, showing both sides empty.

Now, with your right hand, pick up the two coins you just revealed in the top right corner. Put them in your left hand, and then tip them onto the table at the bottom left corner of the square. Withdraw your left hand to the edge of the table and touch your heel to the coin waiting there. With your right hand, pick up the coin at the bottom right corner. Shimmy it into your right palm, display it, then tip your hand over. <u>But retain it in classic palm.</u> Move your left hand forward, with the concealed coin coming too, and cover the two coins at the bottom left corner.

There are, of course, now three coins.

Do the same revealing motion, except your right thumb will not be able to stretch out as much or the classic palmed coin will fall out. Lift your right hand away from the table, then rest it on the edge just in front of you and let the coin fall into your lap. As you do so, pick up the solitary coin from the top left corner with your left hand. Perform the French drop, pretending to take it in your right hand. Put your left hand over the three coins, secretly dropping the finger palmed coin next to them. Put your right hand down, fingers first, at the bottom right corner. Imagine that you've dropped the coin, and then move your hand forward about an inch to cover where the coin would be (and where the spectators think it is). Perform the final reveal as before.

Effect 37

<u>COIN AND GLASS VANISH</u>

Vanishing a glass from a tabletop using a napkin and misdirection is a classic of magic. Here I've put it into a pleasing little routine.

Effect: You place a coin in the middle of a table, cover it with a glass, and cover the glass with a napkin. "Watch! I will make the coin vanish," you proclaim, but when you lift the glass the coin is still there. "The coin hasn't vanished!" But then you give the napkin a flap to show the *glass* has vanished. You put the napkin back in your lap, take the coin and make it vanish at your fingertips. With a flourish, you reproduce the napkin, *and* the glass, *and* the coin, which clinks into the glass.

Method: You need a coin that you can classic palm – I shall use a 2p. Put it on the table. You also need a small glass, like a tumbler. Plastic preferably. And a napkin large enough to cover the glass. Both paper and cloth napkins work fine.

Take the glass tumbler and turn it upside down over the coin. Then cover the glass with the napkin. "Watch; I will vanish the coin." Now take hold of the napkin-covered-glass with your right hand. Don't put your hand beneath the napkin; grasp over the top like in the picture. Lift the napkin-covered-glass off the tabletop, revealing the coin still there.

"Ah! It hasn't vanished!" Whilst everyone's eyes are on the coin, you bring the napkin-covered-glass towards you until it is clear of the tabletop and over your lap. Gesture towards the coin with your left hand as you do this, to distract everyone. Now release a little pressure with your right hand, letting the glass tumbler fall into your lap, but **keeping the glass-shaped mould in the napkin.** If you're male

82

(and if you're reading this book you almost certainly are), be careful of how it lands, okay?

If you're really worried about the glass tumbler tumbling to the floor then you can have your left hand in your lap ready to catch it, but I've never needed to do this.

You can mess with the coin a little with your left fingers as you bring the napkin over with your right hand. The napkin has held the shape of the glass and the spectators assume it is still there. Hold the napkin over the coin, covering it, perform a waving motion over it with your left hand, and then lift it off once more.

The coin is still there. Pretend not to know what's going on. Then laugh and say, "Oh, I know what's happened. It's not the coin that's vanished, it's the glass…" Now comes a nice little flourish. Flick your wrist, throwing the napkin upwards, and grasp one of the corners or edges as it goes. Let it billow out gently. You can do this with your left hand or with both hands if you prefer. Now grasp the napkin with both hands and hold it up by its top corners. Show the front and back and then place it in your lap. Now, what goes on here is important. Whilst putting the napkin in your lap, lift the tumbler the right way up and hold it between your legs. Push one corner of the napkin *inside* the glass. This all happens in one smooth quick motion.

Bring both hands empty back to the coin. "So, the glass has gone," you say, "now to make the coin vanish too." Perform the classic palm vanish, pretending to tip it into your left hand whilst secretly retaining it in right hand classic palm. Close your left hand into a fist. "Watch." Imagine that you throw the coin into the air. That is what you pretend to do. Throw your left hand up and open your fist. Look up, as if watching the coin fly into the air.

Whilst you do this, reach your right hand (with its palmed coin) into your lap. Put your thumb inside the tumbler, against the corner of napkin, and pincer the glass and napkin as one. Lift it out and onto the table – give a little flick of your wrist so the tumbler doesn't end up sitting on the napkin. Now look down to the glass, making exaggerated head movements, as if you've just watched the coin plummet into it. At the same time, release the corner of the napkin and the palmed coin, letting the coin tinkle into the glass.

SECTION TEN

THE DOUBLE LIFT

Possibly *the* greatest utility move in all of card magic. And it does what it says on the tin. In fact, just hearing **double lift** should be an *aha* moment. You turn two cards over as one. This means, when you turn them back over and take the top card, the spectator thinks you're holding the card they've just seen, when really you're holding something else entirely. It's not a basic move (we're well into intermediate territory here, let me tell you), but soooooo worth the effort. There are lots of different types of double lifts, but they're like forces – you just need to be able to execute one decently. We will learn the **double lift from break**.

Double Lift from Break

This one is really all you'll ever need. The disadvantage is you need to catch a break beneath the top two cards beforehand. The advantage is it's surefire.

The get ready: So, how to catch the break. Go pick up a pack now and work through these as I discuss them. *You could:* **1.** Firstly, try spreading the deck face down between your hands. You can do this under the guise of: "Now, you could have chosen any of these cards…" Pinch the top two cards between your right thumb and index finger at the start of the spread. Now, when you close the spread and square the deck, push up against these top two cards with your left fingers and catch a little finger break under them. *Or -* **2.** Hold the deck in left hand mechanic's grip. Right hand comes over, fingers and thumb on the short edges. Push the top two cards over to the right with your left thumb (**pic 1**). Now square them with your right fingers, catching a break under them as you do so. *Or -* **3.** Again, deck in left hand mechanic's grip with right hand gripping short edges, as starting position in 2. Right index finger goes on top of the deck to brace it. Right thumb lifts up two cards from the nearside short edge (**pic 2**). Catch a break beneath them.

Pic 1	Pic 2

The double lift: You have a break beneath the top two cards. Right hand comes over, middle finger at the front, thumb holding *just the two cards above the break.* Index finger on top (**pic 3**). With your right hand, draw the double over to the right. Pretend to push it on its way with your left thumb too, but in reality this thumb doesn't do anything. It's only there for show (**pic 4**). Now pivot the double over, using your left thumb to help (**pic 5**). Place it face-up on the deck, *keeping the break beneath it* (**pic 6**). You can now remove your right hand and do with it what you will.

Pic 3 **Pic 4**

Pic 5 **Pic 6**

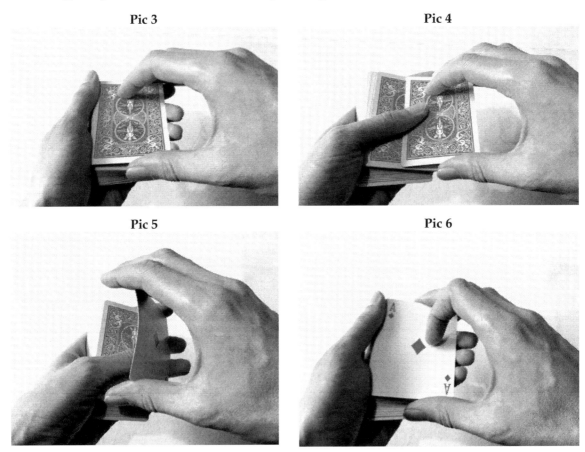

Draw attention to the card (in this example, the ace of diamonds). Now repeat the previous steps, turning the double back over exactly as before, but this time there's no need to keep the break. You can now push over the top card (*and only the top card*) for real with your left thumb and take it between your right fingers. The spectators think it's the ace of diamonds when really it's another card. The ace of diamonds is now the top card of the deck.

There should be no hesitation between the double turning face down again and you pushing off the top card with your left thumb. It should be in one smooth motion.

Effect 38

<u>CLICKER</u>

Effect: The spectator selects a card. You shuffle it back into the pack, then turn over the top card, which is definitely NOT the spectator's card. You take that random card, spread the deck across the table and then run the random card across the spread. It clicks like a wheel of fortune. The spectator stops you, and at that place you turn over the card from the spread. It is not the chosen card. Of course it's not! Because the spectator's card has been in your hand the whole time!

Method: Okay, so a spectator freely selects a card. Now control it to the top using your favourite method. "I have no idea what your card is," you say, and you catch a break beneath the top two cards, "but I can tell you with confidence that *this* is not your card." And perform the double lift, showing a random card to the spectator, who confirms it is not their card. "Absolutely. But we will use it to *find* your card." Turn the double back over and take the *actual* top card, which is their *actual* card. Show the face you must not.

Put the deck in the middle of the table. Using your left hand, spread the cards in a line towards you. "Now, tell me when to stop, whenever you see fit."

Turn the card in your right hand (their card) upright so you're looking at the face and they're looking at the back. Note what it is – let's say it's the ace of diamonds. Now lower one corner to the end of the spread deck (the end nearest you) and begin to run the card down the middle of the spread. You will probably need to hold down the top card to the table with your left hand to stop it moving. It will make a beautiful clicking sound as it goes, just like a wheel of fortune.

They stop you on a card. Nudge away the cards on top of it, making some room, and turn over the card they stopped you on. "Is this your card? No? Oh." Look embarrassed. There may be some laughter, in which case you can say, "I don't know why you're laughing; you got it wrong." It depends. Read the room. Then laugh yourself. "No, I know it's not your card. Because your card is the ace of diamonds." They will stop making fun of you. "And I know it's the ace of diamonds because that is the card in my hand." And reveal it is indeed.

Effect 39

<u>COUNT DETECTOR</u>

Effect: Another teleportation with an added kicker.

Method: Have a card freely selected and then control it to the top. You don't need to know what it is (but the spectator does). Say, "Your card is lost in the deck, but don't worry – we can use this card to help us." And turn over a double from the top of the pack. "Ah, the six of clubs. That will be our count detector." Turn the double back over, take the top card (which is the spectator's chosen card) and put it face-down on the table. They will, of course, believe it is the six of clubs.

"We don't need to worry about the suit, particularly, just the number," you say, and shuffle the top card (six of clubs) to the bottom. Simply peel it off as a single card and then shuffle the rest of the deck onto it. Make sure you don't flash it. "It was a six, wasn't it," you continue, "so we'll count out six cards. Now remember, it could have been anything." And it could have been anything, but it doesn't matter. Whatever number (use 11, 12, 13 for jack, queen, king and 1 for ace), you are simply going to glide back the bottom card (the six of clubs) and peel off the five cards above it, counting out loud as you go. Place them on the table face-down. When you count *six*, you will really take the bottom six of clubs.

Obviously, if you had turned over a jack, you would glide out ten cards and then take the bottom card real jack as the eleventh. And etc.

"What was your card?" you ask, as you hold the six of clubs face-down, and they tell you. "Oh," you say, disappointed. "That's weird. I've somehow got the six of clubs…" and reveal the card you're holding. If you need to, prompt them to turn over the card on the table, which will be their card.

Effect 40

HERE THEN THERE

Here Then There is a very famous teleportation trick where two cards magically change places. Traditionally it requires a duplicate. My version does not.

Effect: Two cards chosen by the spectator magically change places.

Method: The deck can be shuffled. Now say, "This works better when we use one red card and one black card, so please name one black card and one red card." Imagine they say jack of clubs and five of diamonds. Start spreading though the deck, holding it high so only you can see the faces. When you see either the jack of clubs or the five of diamonds you are going to cut the deck at that point so one of those cards goes to the top. Let's say you see the jack of clubs first. Your right hand will lift off all the cards to the right, *including the jack of clubs*, and put them behind the cards in your left hand. This puts the jack of clubs furthest left, which is the top of the deck. You will then spread through again until you see the five of diamonds. Take that card out and put it to the back, atop the jack of clubs. If you can't accomplish that all in your hands put it face-down on the table. Now spread through again and take out any random card. This goes to the back once more, on top of the five of diamonds. Or, face-down onto the table. If you have the two cards face-down on the table you need to put them on top of the deck now. You must end up in this position: a random card on top, five of diamonds, jack of clubs.

Turn a double. It's the five of diamonds. Turn it back over and put the top card (the random card) in front of you. "I'll put the five of diamonds in front of me."

Now turn another double, displaying the jack of clubs. Turn it back over and put the top card (which is the five of diamonds) in front of the spectator. "And the jack of clubs in front of you." They believe the jack of clubs is in front of them and the five of diamonds is in front of you. In reality, they have the five of diamonds and you have the random card. The jack of clubs is still on the top of the deck, which is still in your hand.

With you right hand pick up the random card in front of you. "I take the five of diamonds" [spoiler: not the five of diamonds] "and I'm just going to wave it over your card." Wave it in a slow circle, just as you said you would. Then gesture to the card in front of them. "Turn over that card," you say, and whilst they're doing that you sit back and execute the top change.

They will turn over what they expect to be the jack of clubs, and will find the five of diamonds. You can then reveal that you are now holding the jack of clubs.

Alternative get ready: The set up (and by set up I mean *random card / black / red* at the top of the deck) can be a pain to accomplish. It's not easy to get the random card atop the red/black couple. The process I've put down here (of having the spectator say a red card and black card out loud etc.) is one way. If it's too complicated, simply look through the deck yourself, find a red card next to a black card, and cut the deck one card to the left (so that an indifferent card goes on top of the red/black couple). If you want the spectator to feel like they 'chose' the cards, get the set up ready before hand and riffle force it on the spectator.

Also, it's not even like having contrasting colours is imperative. It just makes the change more visual.

Effect 41

HERE, THERE AND EVERYWHERE

Effect: Two cards chosen by two spectators swap places in an entertaining manner.

Method: This is one of my all time favourites. Have the deck shuffled, then have one spectator pick a card and remember it. Take it back and control it to the top of the deck. Now spread the deck again and have a second spectator pick a card and remember it. You now need to control this card so *both* spectators' cards end up on top of the deck – 1st and 2nd. You can swing cut the deck, offer the packet in your left hand so the 2nd spectator's card goes on top of the 1st spectator's card. Then either false shuffle using an injog, or use a break then cut to table. Or you can use the Marlo tilt, which puts the 2nd spectator's card under the first. <u>And you do need to remember which spectator's card is on top and which is 2nd from top.</u>

Let's imagine you used the Marlo tilt, so the 1st spectator's card is top with the 2nd spectator's card under it. "Your cards are both lost in the deck," you say, and swing cut and catch a break. This puts their chosen cards into the middle, and you're holding a break above them. "But I'm going to say *you* know where your card is," you say to the 2nd spectator (or whoever's card is 2nd from top). "Tell me when to stop." Perform the riffle force. When they stop you, lift up all the cards above the break with your right hand. But instead of offering the left hand packet, put it on top of all the cards in your right hand. This means the deck is exactly how it was before you did the previous swing cut (with the spectators' cards on top).

"What was your card?" you ask. They tell you. Say it's the king of hearts. You turn a double and show the king of hearts. Bemusement will fall all around like snow. You congratulate them. Turn the double back over. Ask them to hold out a hand flat, palm up. Put the top card face-down onto it – remember, they think it is *their* card, but they're now actually holding the 1st spectator's card. "Put your other hand on top of it," you say, "to keep it safe."

Turn to the 1st spectator and perform another swing cut and catch a break. You can either repeat the riffle force section, getting this spectator to stop you, or you can spread through the cards yourself, saying, "I am going to find your card by extrasensory heat perception, which does exist" [it doesn't] "yes, this is it." And you spread through the deck until you feel the break. It takes some effort to spread through the pack whilst holding the break. It isn't easy, but then nothing at this stage is. You need to press against the pack with your left fingers as your thumb spreads or you'll lose it. Anyway, you will be able to feel the break, and the king of hearts will be the next card after it.

Take that card out, or take it off the top of the deck, if you've performed the riffle force. Remember, you are holding the 2nd spectator's card, the king of hearts, and the 2nd spectator is holding the 1st spectator's card, although everyone believes they are holding the king of hearts.

"What was your card?" you ask the 1st spectator. They tell you. Three of spades. You have a look at the card you hold, just you. It's still the king of hearts. Give a kind of hiss. "Would you be impressed if it was a different card?" you say, embarrassed. "Would you be impressed if it was the *king of hearts*, which was *your* card…" And you flick over the card you hold and look pointedly at the 2nd spectator. "Which was the card *you* were holding!"

And, almost certainly without prompting, they will look at the card in their own hand and see they are holding the 1st spectator's card, the three of spades.

Effect 42

<u>THE CLOAK OF INVISIBILITY</u>

Effect: You ask if the spectator likes Harry Potter, and they say of course they do, because who doesn't. They select two cards. You place one card on the floor, and then draw a triangle on the other, which is the symbol for the cloak of invisibility. The spectator says, "But isn't it called the invisi…"

"*Shush!*" you chide. "I can draw a triangle, because you can't copyright a triangle, but let's not push our luck." You take the card with the mark of the cloak of invisibility on it… and it is invisible in your hand. Then you say a magic word and 'lay it down' on top of the card on the floor, where it appears, as if by magic.

Method: The invisible palming concept is an amazing one, and many magicians have developed routines based on it. We will study the 'palm' now. Just from the description, you'll have realised that there is no actual *palm*. The hand is completely empty. You know it's empty and the spectators know it's empty; they're not blind. The illusion, however, is startling. It looks like you take your empty palm and lay a card down on top of another card. The second card just appears on top.

Here's how it works: initially, it looks like you've just put one card down, but you've actually put down two. Then when you lay the 'invisible' card on top, you're simply spreading the two cards. There are a few important details. First, you need to use a surface with friction, like a mat, or a carpet, so that the double doesn't spread when you put it down. Second, the spectators need to be looking directly down, from above, or else they'll probably notice the two cards. So have them standing around a table with a mat – they cannot be *sitting* at the table. Or (and this is how I've always done it) have them on chairs - but not at a table - and perform the effect on the carpet, whilst you sit on the floor. That way you have the friction and you have them looking down on you.

Now go sit on the carpet and pick up your pack. Get a break under the top two cards. Lift the double from the top of the deck by the short edges, with your index finger bowing it slightly to keep it flush, as in **pic 1**. You will place it on the carpet in the same (but reverse) manner. Place the double down, release the edges first and *then* release your index finger from the middle. This ensures the double doesn't spread.

Pic 1

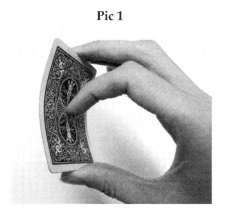

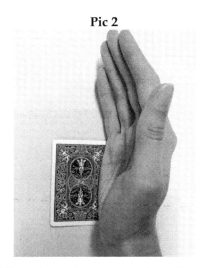

From above, it will look like you put just one card on the carpet. Now, place your right hand along the right edge of the double as in **pic 2.** The edge of your hand is actually on top of the card border.

When you turn your hand over, palm down, the top card of the double will slide slightly across to the right. When you lift off your hand if looks like the card just appears there.

That is the workings of the invisible palm. Neat, huh. Now here is the routine. You need a duplicate card. Use quite a high number card with a good number of pips. This will help you when you come to draw the triangle; the pips act as reference points. Say you use the 8 of hearts. Using permanent marker, draw a triangle on the face of one of the dupes. Make sure the corners hit the pips to make things easier when you come to duplicate it later. If you're a bit wary about producing a perfect duplicate triangle in front of spectators, you can trace a faint outline in pencil on the other 8 of hearts now if you wish.

Now find a card *of opposite colour* (just to make the reveal more startling) and have that on top of the deck. Say it's the 5 of spades. Put the 8 of hearts with the permanent triangle on top of that. Then put the duplicate 8 of hearts without the triangle on top of that, so it becomes the top of the deck. You are ready to wow. Find a spectator(s). Cut the deck and catch a break, preparing for the riffle force. "Do you like Harry Potter?" you ask.

"Of course! Who doesn't?!"

"Quite. Well, you must know about the cloak of invisibility?"

"You mean the invisibility clo…"

"No!" That was close. "The cloak of invisibility. I want to show you how it works, using cards. Tell me when to stop." Perform the riffle force. When they stop you, lift off all the cards above the break with your right hand as normal. Now place the cards in your left hand (the lower half) on top of the pile in your right hand. This puts the force cards on top. You are in this position: naked 8 of hearts; 8 of hearts with triangle; 5 of spades.

Turn over the real top card. "The 8 of hearts," you say, getting out your permanent marker. "Now, the symbol of the cloak of invisibility is a triangle, so I'm going to draw a triangle on the face." Do just that, making it as close to the pre-drawn triangle as you can. Now give it to a spectator to hold and put the marker away.

Now turn a double, displaying the 5 of spades. "I'm going to put this card on the floor [or table, if you're all standing round a table]." Turn it back over *but keep the break*. Now pick up both cards, as one, by the short edges. Flash the face again as you put it on the carpet, face down, in the manner previously mentioned to keep the double flush. Remember, the prepared 8 of hearts is on top.

Take back the 8 of hearts from the spectator and place it on the deck as in the opposite picture, propped up by your thumb. This is known as the *tent vanish*: completely cover the card with your right hand as you say, "I am now going to palm the 8 of hearts… invisibly. All I have to do is say the magic words…" *Izzy Wizzy* or *Oogy Woogy* or *AloHermione*, or whatever, "and the cloak of invisibility is activated!"

Now, under the cover of your right hand, simply let the tented 8 of hearts fall flush with the rest of the deck. Lift your right hand, curled slightly as if you have a card palmed there, and bring it in front of the spectators. Keep it palm down as you say, "Do you see the card in my hand?" Of course they don't. Now turn your hand over, displaying your empty palm. "Do you see the card now?"

They will look confused, maybe laugh a little. "It is there," you assure them. "It's just wearing the cloak of invisibility. But watch, if I lay it down the cloak comes off and it becomes visible again."

And 'lay' the card down as mentioned previously. It will 'appear' on top of the 5 of spades, and you will be able to turn both cards over. The fact that the 8 of hearts is 'signed' with the triangle really adds to the illusion.

Effect 43

<u>A TRIO OF CHANGES</u>

Effect: A three-point routine involving the transformation of indifferent cards into the spectator's signed chosen card.

The Classic Colour Change

The second transformation in this routine utilizes the *classic colour change*, which is slick and visual. It usually works best if the two cards are red and black rather than the same colour, but in this routine it doesn't matter so much because the signature acts as a strong visual aid. Anyway, let's learn the mechanics.

Take the deck and turn over a double on top. Let it lie flush. Now draw attention to the face up card on show. Do this by pushing it forward with the flat of your right palm, so that it overhangs (**pic 1**, side view). Now press the heel of your hand down against the card *below it*, second from top, which you have uncovered. Draw your hand back to uncover the top face card, sliding the second card backwards (**pic 2**). This is hidden by the back of your hand. Slide the second card until it is completely free of the top card. Push down with the heel of your hand, tilting the second card up like a seesaw. Now slide it forward again, *over* the top card (**pic 3**).

Pic 1

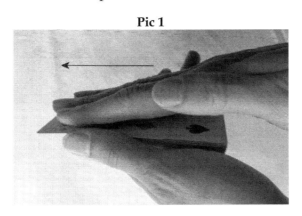

Pic 2

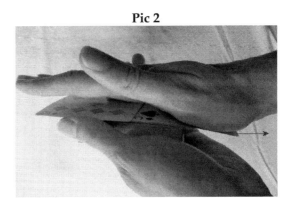

Pic 3

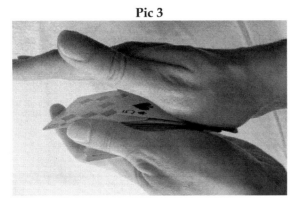

With your **left** index finger, push the card still protruding over the front of the deck (the original top card, which the spectators have been looking at) backwards so it's flush with the rest of the pack. Your right hand is still covering the entire deck. What you have done is exchange the top card for the second card without anyone noticing.

Now suddenly spread your right fingers and draw your hand away, revealing the change. It is a very strong and visual change.

Method: Now that we have learnt the classic colour change we can get on with the effect. You can be standing or sitting, but you need a table nearby. Have a spectator freely choose a card and sign it. Now apparently lose it in the deck but really control it to the top. "I'm not exactly sure where your card is, but I'm pretty sure it's not this one." And turn over a double on top, keeping a break beneath it. It is just a random card. Get the spectator to put out a hand, palm up. Then turn the double back over and take the real top card, which is the spectator's card. Put it face down in the spectator's palm and get them to sandwich it with their other hand. "Press down hard and think of your card," you say, which rhymes. "Now… have a look."

They'll discover the random card has turned into their signed card. Take it back and once more pretend to lose it into the deck whilst actually controlling it to the top. If you can, use a different method. Once again turn over a double but this time leave it flush on top. "We can make this much more visual by doing it face-up."

Perform the classic colour change. That is change number two. Now catch a break beneath the top two cards. You will have to do this with a thumb count, as you can't spread the cards (they're face-up). Turn the double over, face-down, and take the real top card. The spectators think it is the signed card but it is actually a random one. Put it face-down on a table, or any appropriate surface. Now you will 'dribble' the rest of the pack on top of it for the third and final change.

Random card on table

Pack held 10cm above

Hold the deck in your right hand as in the opposite picture; by the short edges, from above, with your index finger on top. Hold it about 10cm above the face-down card on the table.

Now apply a little pressure with your index finger, bowing the deck slightly. Let the cards fall from the bottom in a trickle by gently relaxing your pincer grip on the short edges.

It takes a little practise but is not hugely difficult. Note that this is the *dribble*, not the card 'spring', which **is** difficult. You are going to dribble off the deck in a steady stream onto the tabled card. But do *not* let the top card fall. Dribble off every other card but retain the top card, which if you remember is their chosen card. You can then reveal that, once again, that you hold their signed card.

Effect 44

<u>FORGET-ME-NOT</u>

Effect: A feat of mentalism I came up with using only the double lift and a lot of showmanship. A spectator picks a card and remembers it. Then you, with help from the other spectators, make her forget that card and implant a totally different card in her mind. She is convinced this second card is the one she originally saw.

Method: The deck can be freely shuffled. Ask for a volunteer, then lead her a few feet away from the rest of the spectators. Let's imagine she's called Angelina. She should turn round so she's facing them. "This is a tricky feat of mentalism," you say. "It doesn't always work…" [it does] "…but we will do our best. Just try to follow my instructions the best you can, okay?"

Take the deck and ask Angelina to give it one last shuffle. "Happy the cards are mixed? You can give it a cut too, if you like." Maybe she does. Retrieve the deck. "I'm going to show you and *only you* the top card," you tell her. Stand in front of her, with your back to the other spectators so they can't see the deck. Turn a double. Let's say it's the three of clubs. "Have a look at your card and remember it. It's very important. Are you clear what your card is?"

She nods. Turn the double back over and pick up the top card, which she will assume is hers. Let your deck hand fall to your side and say, "I want you to say the name of your card over and over *but only in your head. Nothing out loud, okay? Do that now."* You turn to the other spectators. "The rest of you, *this* is her card. But again, don't say anything out loud." You are facing the spectators, so when you hold up the random card Angelina won't see it and notice it's not the three of clubs. Glimpse this card – let's imagine it's the king of hearts – then hand it to another spectator. "Hold it facing you." Obviously don't let Angelina see it.

"What we're going to do," you say to the spectators, "is look at the next card in the pack. Don't say anything out loud…" You turn over the top card on the deck, which is the three of clubs. "Everybody see it? Okay, we're going to make Angelina *forget* the card she's thinking of. Then we're going to make her believe *this* is her actual card using just our minds."

Sounds impossible, but they don't know Angelina's card *is already* the three of clubs. It was never the king of hearts. You can let another spectator take the three of clubs, as long as they keep it to themselves.

"Angelina, I want you to keep saying the name of your card to yourself, over and over. I'm going to make you forget it, although you won't know it."

Now, if you wish you can take the king of hearts, put it face up on top of the deck and perform the classic colour change (page 90), as a visual representation of 'her' card disappearing from her mind. Obviously, keep your back to Angelina as you do this so she doesn't see. "Watch the king of hearts," you say to the spectators, "as it disappears completely." And it does disappear, beneath the face down top card of the deck. As I said, this step is optional.

"Angelina, I want you to keep saying the name of your card to yourself as I do this. I am going to now make you forget the name of your card. But I am also going to implant the name of another card into your head. It will be painless. Please hold out your hand."

You lightly touch one of her fingers. "There! I think it worked. Believe it or not, the name of the card you are repeating to yourself is now *not* the card you first saw. I'll prove it. Please say the name of your card out loud."

She says the three of clubs, which will amaze the spectators, who believe she saw the king of hearts. And it will also confuse Angelina, who is *sure* it was the three of clubs she first saw when you turned that double.

SECTION ELEVEN

THE STOOGE MAGICIAN PRINCIPLE

In magic, a *stooge* plays the part of a spectator when in fact he is the magician's accomplice. The stooge is different to the magician's assistant, because the audience knows that the assistant is in on the magic. A stooge pretends to be part of the audience, just another spectator, when in fact they are a part of the trick.

When mentalists such as Derren Brown choose random spectators from the audience, they may do so by throwing a Frisbee or a ball into the stalls. This is to demonstrate to everyone that the choice *is* random, and that the spectators who come up on stage are not stooges.

Many magicians (most?) do not use stooges or even particularly like the idea of stooges. They consider it a kind of 'cheat'. I have sympathy with this view. Indeed, I've never actually used a stooge myself. The argument 'for' stooges can be made thus: "Of course using a stooge is cheating and lying… but everything we do is cheating and lying. We're upfront about our cheating and lying from the very start – that's why we call ourselves illusionists and call our magic 'tricks' – and the audience *expects* us to cheat and lie to them."

If you're uneasy about the idea of using a stooge, that's absolutely fine. You might want to skip this section. But maybe not. Because this concept of mine isn't about *using* a stooge… It's about *becoming* a stooge yourself.

You, the magician, are going to pretend to be a member of the audience. *You* are the stooge. In this scenario, the guy holding the cards doing the magic is not actually a magician. He's just some guy you know. He doesn't need any kind of magical skill, just the ability to hold a pack of cards. He doesn't even need to be able to shuffle. What he does need to be able to do is remember his lines. And be able to *act* like a magician.

You will be milling around somewhere in public, near a group of strangers. Your friend, the guy who's playing the part of the magician (shall we call him Magic Mike? Let's call him Magic Mike), he'll approach the big group of strangers and say, "Guys, can I show you some magic?"

Hopefully they'll say yes and won't run him out of town. Magic Mike will take out his cards, which you've probably lent him. You will expertly merge with the group, becoming one of the spectators.

Magic Mike will give the cards to one of the strangers and have them inspected, shuffled, whatever. Then he will take them back. And he will turn to you, and you will pretend you've never seen each other before. And then you will both perform the routine listed here, which you will have practised together, and which you both know off by heart. You are performing for the group of strangers, of course. They are the real spectators, and they will be blown away.

Effect 45

<u>THE AMBITIOUS CARD ROUTINE</u>

This routine is one of the staples in card magic. A spectator's chosen and signed card magically jumps to the top of the deck in mysterious and entertaining ways. There are of course many ways to do this as an *actual* magician, but not like this.

When I was at university a magician came into our Students Union and performed this on me (not knowing I was a budding magician myself). This is when I first had the idea of the *stooge magician*.

One of the main advantages to this principle is that of the duplicate signature. A card with a lot of pips makes things easier, like a seven or an eight, as the pips give reference points and make copying your signature easier. Of course, by signature we just mean your first name. In theory, you could make up a name that is the easiest to write and copy. Like 'Matt'. That's my name, but it's also quite a good one to duplicate. Lots of straight lines. It might not work so well if you're a girl, I guess. Try something like *Lila*, or *Anna*, in that case.

In the safety of your own home, write your chosen name on the face of a card. Say it's the seven of hearts. Notice where each line falls in relation to the pips. Now get a duplicate seven of hearts and, in pencil, faintly trace a copy of your name on it. Try to make it as exact a copy as you can. During the trick, you will trace these faint pencil lines with permanent marker.

Put the original card, the one signed in black marker, in an envelope and put it in your pocket. Now give an identical envelope to Magic Mike for him to put in his pocket. Put the pencil-signed seven of hearts in the pack anywhere. Put the pack in its box and give to Magic Mike. You are all set.

You have infiltrated the group of strangers and Magic Mike has given out the cards to be shuffled. He takes them back and turns to you. "Hi, what's your name?"

"Matt." You say the name on the signed card in the envelope in your pocket. Please don't say any other name, alright?

"Matt," says Magic Mike, and he hands you the pack. "Can you look through the deck and pick out any card. Any one you like."

Sounds fair. You spread through the pack. Try to look a little clumsy, and not as if you're perfectly at home with a deck in your hand. Take out the seven of hearts. It has your pencil marks on, remember? Faint enough so no one else will notice.

"I want you to write your name on the card," Magic Mike says. He has got out his permanent marker. "Lean it on the top of the deck, yes, like that."

You trace the pencil lines, using the deck for support, creating a perfect duplicate of the signed card in the envelope in your pocket.

"Great." Magic Mike takes back the marker. "So, you've signed this seven of hearts, making it one of a kind. Happy?"

Tee hee. You say you are happy.

"Good. Now, turn over the card and shuffle it into the deck."

You turn your signed card face down (the rest of the cards are face down too). You need to false shuffle the deck so that the signed card ends up <u>second from the top</u>. Lift off the bottom half of the deck in your right hand (like you would for any overhand shuffle), peel off one card on top of your signed card, then in jog the next card. Now complete the false shuffle with injog, bringing your signed card second to top.

"So," says Magic Mike. "Your card is lost in there."

"Yes." No.

"Turn over the top card."

You turn over the actual top card, which is random.

"That's not your card." Magic Mike states the obvious. "Turn it back over."

You turn it back over, face down. Now Magic Mike puts one hand over the deck and holds it there, and as he does so you get ready to turn a double, catching a break beneath the top two cards. He removes his hand and says, "Turn it over again. Look what's happened."

You turn over the double, displaying your signed card. Gasp.

"Turn it back over," Magic Mike says, and you turn the double face down. "Pick it up."

You take the *top* card, keeping the face hidden from the spectators, as it is not your signed card (though they believe it is). Magic Mike says to one of the other spectators, "Pick up about half the deck."

The spectator takes the top half of the deck from you and holds it. Remember, she has the signed card on top of her pile. Magic Mike says, "We're just going to work with half the deck now." To you: "Put your card in the remainder of the deck."

It's a random card you've got, remember. You put it in the half-deck you're holding, and Magic Mike tells you to shuffle it. He waves his hand over the top of your half. "Turn over the top card."

You turn it over, and of course it is just a random card. He does it again, same outcome. "You see," Magic Mike says, "that is *not* the top of the deck." He points to the half-deck in the other spectator's hand. "*That* is the top of the deck." She turns over her top card, which is the signed card. It is an impressive reveal.

"Okay." Magic Mike takes the half-deck from the spectator and gives it back to you so you have the complete deck. Then he takes the signed card and hands that to you too. "This time I want you to put in your card *face-up*, in the middle of the deck."

You have turned and faced the rest of the spectators, watching the previous reveal. So you are at the perfect angle to Marlo Tilt your signed card in second from the top, face-up.

"This will be far more visual," Magic Mike says, "because your card is face-up. You will see it appear. Watch carefully. I'm going to cover the deck with both hands."

Magic Mike puts both hands over the deck. Remember, your face-up card is underneath the top card. The deck is in your left hand, and your right hand is cupping it also. You need both hands to work this next sleight.

As soon as Magic Mike covers the deck, you peel the top card sideways (to the left) with your left thumb. This allows you to slide out, sideways to the right, your signed card from beneath it with your right thumb. Then square the deck, sliding your face-up card on top. It is basically a sideways version of the classic colour change. Magic Mike hides the small motions you make with his hands. When you have completed the sleight you can give him a sign. Maybe cough, or laugh or something. He withdraws his hands, slowly, revealing the face-up card has appeared on top.

The last reveal is the most powerful. You've guessed it – it makes use of the duplicate signed card in the envelope in your pocket. Magic Mike himself takes the pack and inserts your signed card into it anywhere and, if he has the ability, shuffles the deck. The signed card is really lost in there. He can give it to another spectator to shuffle if he wants, before giving it to you once more. "Shuffle the deck as well," he instructs. You do so. "Now turn over the top card."

It is, of course, a random card. Probably. There's a 1/52 chance it'll be your signed seven of hearts, and that would be hilarious, but hopefully it'll just be a random card. Magic Mike tells you to pick up that random top card. Let's say it's the three of diamonds.

He pulls an envelope out of his pocket. It's identical to the envelope in your pocket. He shows it empty. Then he takes the three of diamonds off you. "I put the top card of the deck into the envelope, see?" He puts it inside and shows everyone. Then he seals the envelope and hands it to you. "Put it in your pocket for now."

You take it and put it in the same pocket that has the other, original, prepared envelope. Remember whether it goes in front of or behind the original envelope. Magic Mike takes the deck from you. "We don't need the rest of these cards now." He puts them back into their card box and stashes it in an inside pocket away from prying eyes. "Watch." He puts one hand over his own pocket and extends his other hand towards your pocket. Hopefully the one with the envelope(s) in. Then he relaxes. "Take out the envelope."

You need to take out the original prepared envelope, okay? Not the one you've just stashed away with the three of diamonds. The other one, with the duplicate signed seven of hearts.

"Open it," says Magic Mike, and you do, and it blows everyone's mind.

APPENDIX

FURTHER MATERIAL

The first thing I'll recommend (and I hope you forgive me for doing so) is my own Book Test: **MERCURY**. It's a physical book, and every double page spread is the same (it's like a one-way forcing deck, but in book form). The spectator can open the book anywhere. You run your finger down the page and they stop you on a word. The word is *happening*, and it matches a prediction you've had in an envelope the whole time. Available for £10 on Amazon, under the pseudonym LM Wood.

As far as *Mentalism* goes, you should definitely purchase a **NAIL WRITER** (also called a **swami** gimmick). This nifty little thing is a pencil lead that attaches to your nail, allowing you to secretly write predictions after the fact.

I also highly recommend **LOOPS** by Yigal Mesika. These are little loops of invisible thread that go around your wrist, allowing you to seemingly move objects with your mind.

As far as card magic goes, there are lots of gimmicked decks: one-way forcing, stripper (ooh-er), Svengali, marked… but the one I would recommend above all others is the **INVISIBLE DECK**. It's not an actual invisible deck, mind. The spectator can name ANY card, and this special gimmicked deck allows you to reveal their card (whichever one they chose) face-down in a face-up spread.

AFTERWORD

I hope you have enjoyed this book. If you have, please leave a review on Amazon! As a small publisher, reviews are really important to us.

Perhaps I'll do a sequel. *HOW TO DO MAGIC: Professional Effects For The Intermediate Illusionist.* Something like that.

Look out for it, maybe.

Anyway, thanks for buying. I hope magic brings you as much pleasure as it has brought me.

INDEX OF SLEIGHTS

Printed in Great Britain
by Amazon

35607073R00058